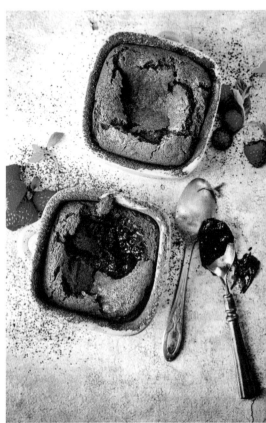

Lucy Bee

COCONUT OIL
RECIPES FOR REAL LIFE

Over 100 recipes to share with friends and family,
using nature's perfect ingredients

Photography by Dan Jones

quadrille

PUBLISHING DIRECTOR Sarah Lavelle
COMMISSIONING EDITOR Lisa Pendreigh
PROJECT EDITOR Amy Christian
COPY EDITOR Sally Somers
CREATIVE DIRECTOR Helen Lewis
ART DIRECTION AND DESIGN Katherine Keeble
PHOTOGRAPHER Dan Jones
FOOD STYLIST Bianca Nice
PROPS STYLIST Holly Bruce
HAIR AND MAKE-UP Maria Comparetto
PRODUCTION DIRECTOR Vincent Smith
PRODUCTION CONTROLLER Emily Noto

First published in 2016 by
Quadrille Publishing Limited

Text © 2016 Lucy Bee Ltd
Photography © 2016 Dan Jones
Design and layout © 2016 Quadrille Publishing Ltd

Quadrille is an imprint of Hardie Grant
www.hardiegrant.com.au

Quadrille Publishing Ltd
Pentagon House
52–54 Southwark Street
London SE1 1UN
www.quadrille.co.uk

Cataloguing in Publication Data: a catalogue record for this book is available from the British Library.

ISBN: 978 1 84949 889 0

Printed in China

MIX
Paper from
responsible sources
FSC® C008047

COCONUT OIL: RECIPES FOR REAL LIFE

It feels like just yesterday that the team and I sat down to tackle our first book, *Coconut Oil: Nature's Perfect Ingredient,* and we're just as amazed and excited for this, our second cookery book. So here I am with my daily cup (or rather soup-bowlful!) of cacao hot chocolate, ready to welcome you to book two, *Coconut Oil: Recipes for Real Life.*

For so many of us now, life is extremely busy and at times very demanding, which can make it tricky to stay on track and cook from scratch. With so many options out there, like microwave meals (which are often full of secret sugars and 'nasties') and takeaway services, it can sometimes be all too easy to go for these quick fixes.

That said, many people are also becoming increasingly more conscious of what they put into their body. I've really noticed this on social media, where I spend A LOT of my time (if you hadn't noticed). Nowadays, you're more likely to see people hitting the gym or sharing photos of their latest food creations than posting pictures of themselves out in a club. That's why, after sitting around our kitchen table brainstorming (and eating Salted Caramel Fudge, see page 154) the title *Recipes for Real*

'IT'S ABOUT MAKING HEALTHY EATING SECOND NATURE IN YOUR REAL LIFE.'

Life seemed the perfect fit. Because that's just it — it's about making healthy eating second nature to you in real life.

The aim of this book is to help you in your everyday cooking. It's important we fuel our body with nutritious, filling foods that will help to make us feel our best. A quote that always sticks in my mind is: 'When you eat rubbish, you feel rubbish.' That's why throughout this book you'll see that we only use ingredients that are as close to nature as possible.

You will also notice that all the recipes are gluten-free; this is because I'm a coeliac. I was diagnosed at 18 months old and this has naturally led me to be very health conscious. Although I am not a nutritionist it's something I feel very passionately about and I'm constantly researching ingredients to see what exactly they are doing for my body.

KEEPING FAIR TRADE IN MIND
The title of this book, *Recipes for Real Life*, really has a double meaning. In the more obvious sense, it's about making nutritious meals that are 'down to earth' and don't involve a whole host of ingredients unknown to many of us.

In another important way, it's about choosing products that support the real lives of those involved in the production process. If you're familiar with Lucy Bee, you may already know how important it is to us that our ingredients are Fair Trade certified.

'SOCIAL RESPONSIBILITY IS AT THE HEART OF THE LUCY BEE BRAND. WHEN YOU BUY OUR PRODUCTS, YOU KNOW YOU ARE MAKING A DIFFERENCE.'

The discussion of Fair Trade usually revolves around fair pay for the workers. However, we want to look at this in another way, and instead think about what happens if we don't purchase Fair Trade products.

The concept of zero child labour, safe working conditions, contracts for all and a fair wage may seem like automatic rights for most of us, but this isn't a certainty in some parts of the world, for workers who aren't part of a Fair Trade scheme. We care passionately about this and are very aware of our social responsibility as a company, so in the same way that we're mindful of the kind of foods that we are eating, we're also very mindful of the hearts and hands behind the scenes.

I occasionally get asked if animals such as monkeys are used to harvest our coconuts, as this is a topic that has cropped up now and again in the media. The answer is 'No!'. Our certification body, the Fair Trade Sustainability Alliance (FairTSA) guarantees that this does not happen. It's scenarios like this, that you wouldn't necessarily even think of, that show how important it is to buy into Fair Trade products wherever possible. I mean, before importing coconut oil, I never would have thought that in some places monkeys were kept in cages and used to collect coconuts!

I have been lucky enough to make a trip to the Dominican Republic to visit the producers of our cacao powder and to see behind the scenes of one of my favourite products. This is something I've always wanted to do and it will be amazing to see in the future how the local community will benefit from your Fair Trade contributions.

Having spoken to our producers, their main goal is to set up an extended education centre for children in the community. One thing they will be taught is to speak English, which should boost their job prospects in the future, as tourism is a large source of income for the Dominican Republic.

ALLERGY INFORMATION

If, like me, you have a particular food intolerance then you will be forever checking packaging and labels to decipher what you can and can't eat. To make your cooking choices easier, each of the recipes in this book is accompanied by a symbol – or symbols – denoting the suitability of the dish for people following specific diets. Below is an at-a-glance guide to what each of those symbols stands for:

GF Gluten-free **DF** Dairy-free

WF Wheat-free **V** Vegan

LF Lactose-free **VEG** Vegetarian

COOKING WITH COCONUT OIL

Those of you who have read our first cookbook will be familiar with our tips on cooking with coconut oil, so apologies if you've already heard this! Here, we will hopefully give all you new converts to coconut oil some advice that we've picked up ourselves along the way.

I sound like a broken record saying this (and everyone who knows me tells me I do!) but a little goes a long way. One teaspoon of coconut oil is the general rule when frying a small quantity of ingredients and you can use it as a replacement for all processed oils. Don't panic, though! It doesn't make all your food taste of coconut. The flavour is generally lost when heated and instead it just enhances the taste of the other ingredients. You tend to only taste coconut when you've used too much (it's ok – it happens sometimes).

Coconut oil is a medium-chain fatty acid (MCFA), a saturated fat that the body deals with incredibly efficiently. We opt for the unrefined kind, which is as natural and unprocessed as can be (extra virgin) as well as raw, organic and Fair Trade. The oil is extracted within one to four hours of the coconut being cracked open and is naturally white and clear, with a coconut aroma. This is versus those that are refined, bleached and deodorized, a necessary procedure when coconuts are split and left out in the elements for days before the oil is extracted; often the flesh can be mouldy and produce a brown coloured oil.

KEEP WISE AND ORGANIZE!
Planning ahead is a very important factor in a healthy lifestyle. My family and I always cook extra – it's something we have got into the habit of doing and it often stops me from snacking on unhealthier things. One great idea is to cook a big batch of sweet potatoes. These work so well in omelettes, salads, or – a particular favourite of mine – as a jacket sweet potato; if you haven't tried this, I highly recommend it. Or, if you are making pasta one evening, make enough to have for lunch the day after.

What's really key is to not be wasteful. Our recipes here should be seen as simple guidelines that allow you to adapt them based on which ingredients you've got in the house. Run out of chickpeas? Throw in some cannellini beans instead! The same can be said for meat and fish. Buying whatever fish or meat is available at the fresh food counter or fishmonger/butcher can save you some cash: opt for cheaper cuts if they're on offer.

'OUR LUCY BEE COCONUT OIL IS RAW, ORGANIC AND FAIR TRADE. WHAT'S NOT TO LOVE?'

'MODERATION IS THE KEY – WE ALL DESERVE A TREAT. DON'T BE TOO HARD ON YOURSELF.'

Buying organic products is another important way to shop for me. The number of genetically modified organisms (GMOs) used in farming today is alarming, as is the number of pesticides sprayed onto our food. That is why I prefer to find organic produce where I can.

That said, it's not always possible to buy everything organic, so it might be worth noting the following items that, if possible, should always be bought as organic produce because they have the most pesticides sprayed onto them. These are:

✦ Apples
✦ Strawberries
✦ Celery
✦ Peaches
✦ Cucumbers
✦ Spinach
✦ Courgettes (zucchini)
✦ Tomatoes
✦ (Bell) peppers
✦ Collard greens

I'm very lucky that both my parents are brilliant cooks and on many occasions when they would cook me gluten-free versions of meals as a child, my friends would still want to eat mine! Of course, I gave them a bite – but only one. One of my favourite childhood recipes is the classic Pizza (see page 92) which I have adapted so that it's a lot simpler to make.

I have always had an interest in cooking but haven't always had as much confidence as I would have liked. Timings tend to be an issue for me. I feel like I either have all the time in the world or none at all. But since our first cookbook, that has completely changed. I now love cooking and experimenting with flavours, textures, gadgets and recipes. I am more of a 'quick cook' and like to spend as little time in the kitchen as possible, and this is reflected in a lot of the recipes here – achievable in a short amount of time but still full of mouth-watering flavours. There are also some longer recipes when you do have a little more time to spend in the kitchen. Food is here to enjoy, so it's important to choose what you are cooking wisely and feel happy with the end result!

GETTING BACK ON TRACK

I'm a huge believer that life is about balance and moderation. It's easy on social media to show a perfect life full of clean foods, regular exercise and lots of water – but that's not always the reality. We are only human, after all, and want to enjoy life; we can be way too hard on ourselves.

The pressure of looking good can make us feel unhappy. I find when this happens, I end up bingeing and then feeling angry with myself for doing so. What I am trying to get at here is, if there is a day you want to eat, say, three burgers, two portions of chips and a couple of frozen strawberry daiquiris or glasses of wine, then do it and enjoy every minute! Then tell yourself you need to get back on track by planning your meals. Life is here to be lived, not to be constantly on a diet. By eating as close to nature as possible, your body will love you, and when you eat the right thing, you can actually eat lots of it (well, in moderation)!

When you feel like you've fallen off the healthy wagon, and the wagon is already halfway across the world, just stop and take a minute to think about your personal reasons for getting back on track. Could it be an event coming up? Just simply feeling tired and unmotivated? Holiday approaching soon? If that's the case, I thought I would share some of my favourite tips for when this happens. I hope you find them helpful too.

✦ **Prep and plan.** This really does make life easier for you in the long run.

✦ **Write a food diary.** This is really useful, especially when feeling bloated, puffy or not your best. Write down everything you eat for a week and describe how you feel each day. If you eat something on one of those days and feel bloated and uncomfortable then try eliminating it to see if you feel better without it. Even though you haven't got a food allergy, it doesn't mean you aren't sensitive to certain foods.

✦ **Make your list your screensaver.** This one is quite random but what I find useful is to write down my goals in my notepad on my phone, screenshot it, and make it my background. For example, drinking two litres (four pints) of water or doing 100 squats a day (nice try, Lucy!). Sounds silly but it really works for me.

✦ **Get fruity or spicy with your water.** We all know the importance of staying hydrated but sometimes don't drink enough water. I love to add different ingredients to mine to make it taste good. Try ginger, lemon, mint, orange, pineapple, or different herbs and fruit.

✦ **Hot drinks.** Try drinking herbal teas, green or fruity teas, turmeric lattes and cacao hot chocolates.

✦ **Start each morning with warm lemon water.** This is great at detoxing your digestive system and removing waste products from your body that have accumulated, which is why I like to have it first thing in the morning. You may be surprised to learn that although lemons are very acidic, when digested they become alkaline, helping to balance the body's pH levels.

✦ **Work out with a friend.** We all love to have a good catch up with our friends, so why not do this on a long walk somewhere? Working out with friends is a brilliant way of getting your fitness in as well as having a chat. I find you encourage each other, too.

✦ **Simple swaps.** This is just a bit of fun but does make a difference. Think of healthier alternatives, for example:

- ✔ Homemade juices over shop-bought ones
- ✔ Carrots and celery with hummus over bread
- ✔ Cacao hot chocolate over sugar-laden hot chocolate
- ✔ Homemade granola over sugar-filled store-bought granola
- ✔ Homemade almond milk over store-bought almond milk
- ✔ Climbing the stairs rather than taking the lift

TIP

Follow my steps for creating good habits and you will soon be back on track and feeling motivated – I promise!

Coconut Oil

Himalayan Salt

Lucuma Powder

Turmeric Powder

Cinnamon Powder

Maca Powder

Cacao Powder

ALL ABOUT LUCY BEE

If you're new to Lucy Bee, I thought you might like to know a little more about us. We're a family-run business and I am one of three siblings. My sister, Daisy, is currently studying for a Masters degree in Public Health Nutrition in London and my brother, Jack, is living and definitely loving the life as a university student in Newcastle. My dad, Phil, is the businessman behind Lucy Bee and he has a background in importing brown rice pasta, while my mum, Natalie, helps in all different areas of the business.

Then there is me, Lucy, the coeliac. Well that's not my job title but it's the reason Lucy Bee came about, and is why my name is on the brand. My dad based it on how I live my life, so I originally started off by doing social media. When I was first asked to make a Twitter account for coconut oil, I replied, 'Who is going to follow a jar of coconut oil and how do I go about this?'. I just started posting photos of my food, random tips, memes, quotes or anything I found interesting that fitted into health and wellbeing, and over time our social media platforms started to grow.

I am also a qualified beauty therapist, and am currently still practising one day a week. Those who know about coconut oil will already know how it's the perfect beauty product, which I will talk about in more detail later.

The Lucy Bee team has grown over the last year, with a small office full of coconut-crazy and superfood-loving people. We've added to our range of ingredients too, all of which are things that I use all the time.

So, I think that now is the perfect time to introduce you all to our new range of Lucy Bee ingredients:

LUCY BEE CACAO POWDER

Firstly, I have to confess my addiction to this. When I say I have a cacao hot chocolate every single day, I mean it. All you need to do is whiz it up with some almond milk and warm through and you're done. I've also found it's the trick to stopping myself from reaching for treats after dinner — its rich taste curbs my sweet tooth.

Our cacao powder comes from the Dominican Republic and our producers, Gabriela and Daniel, form a team with a group of dedicated, young single mothers to help bring it to you.

For those of you not familiar with cacao, the plant grows on trees in areas like the 'cacao belt' in the centre of the Dominican Republic. The beans are found inside cacao pods, which can be extremely vibrant in colour, ranging from red to green to yellow. In the case of our cacao, Criollo and Forastero beans are collected, roasted and milled to a fine powder. The roasting process only reaches a maximum temperature of 45°C/113°F to ensure it can still be considered raw.

LUCY BEE CINNAMON POWDER

This was something I was really excited to bring out, because cinnamon is a huge staple in my kitchen. I find it in almost every dessert recipe nowadays too! We import our cinnamon from India and work with farmers who are trained in organic, sustainable farming methods.

There are two main types of cinnamon, Ceylon and Cassia. Cassia cinnamon is what you'll most likely come across in a supermarket, whereas our cinnamon powder is Ceylon, otherwise known as 'true cinnamon', with a sweet, subtle flavour.

Ceylon cinnamon is also highly valued for cooking and medicinal purposes. Our producers place a great importance on organic farming methods, which is why we are proud to say our cinnamon powder is GMO- and pesticide-free, as well as being Fair Trade.

LUCY BEE LUCUMA POWDER

This is made from a fruit, which is cleaned and peeled, pitted, sliced, dried and then milled to a fine powder before it's ready to be packaged up. It's most often used in desserts and sweet treats but has a low glycaemic index. It has a subtle maple flavour to it, so it's really delicious when added to recipes like banana ice cream or our Salted Caramel Fudge (see page 154). It's similar to maca powder, in that many people like adding it to smoothies for a sweet taste.

Our lucuma powder is a raw, organic, Fair Trade product that comes all the way from Peru and is woven into its history there. Known previously as the 'gold of the Incas', it has been discovered at archaeological excavation sites. I find it amazing how it was used all those years ago and now we play a part in bringing it to you, thousands of miles away!

LUCY BEE MACA POWDER

Our maca powder is from the Jauja province of Peru, the same area as our lucuma, and we were amazed at the history behind this product when we were first introduced to it. It was considered a treasured food source by Incan warriors, who would often consume it before going into battle (sounds pretty amazing, right?). The powder is a blend of black, red and white maca roots and is also organic and Fair Trade certified. Simply add it to smoothies and desserts to give a subtle sweet flavour.

Our maca powder goes through something called gelatinisation, which removes the starch content, making it easier for your body to absorb the nutrients. These nutrients are in abundance and include amino acids, iodine, iron, potassium, B vitamins and vitamin C.

LUCY BEE TURMERIC POWDER

A flavoursome and nutrient-packed powder, turmeric has long been a popular ingredient in Indian cooking. It has a vibrant orange

'OUR PRODUCTS ARE AS CLOSE TO NATURE AS POSSIBLE.'

colour and appears all over the internet in blogs and recipes, including in spice-infused drinks like turmeric latte: turmeric and other spices (I like cardamom pods, vanilla extract and cinnamon) added to almond milk with a little coconut oil, black pepper and honey, (which is optional to sweeten) and warmed up makes such a delicious drink.

If you're unfamiliar with turmeric, it has a slightly peppery taste with a hint of orange (go figure) and ginger – it's actually part of the ginger root family.

We love adding turmeric to our soups or sprinkled over roasted broccoli and cauliflower. But, did you know it's also got a pretty impressive reputation as a beauty product? It's said to be great for acne, and can be used to make a face mask. I have to warn you though, turmeric can stain your skin if you're not careful – and you don't want to look like you've overdone it with the fake tan! However, I mix it with yoghurt and I've never had any issues with it staining.

EPSOM SALTS, HIMALAYAN SALT AND DEAD SEA SALTS

I seriously swear by these products. I have been using bath salts for years and I really believe in their benefits. I mean, who doesn't love an excuse to soak in the bath for 20 minutes? A lot of people are deficient in magnesium because they lack it in their diet and don't know what the best sources are. Epsom salts contain the highest level of magnesium of all three salts, and you may have heard of them being used after a workout for your muscles.

Dead Sea salts are similar to this and, like Epsom salts, are used only for beauty purposes (so I'd better not catch you eating any!).

Himalayan salt is a bit different in that you can use it for both cooking and beauty, so we won't think you're mad if you've got some in your kitchen and bathroom!

All of our salts combine perfectly with coconut oil to make a homemade body scrub. You can add in a drop or two of essential oils to take it one step further, too.

COCONUT OIL AND ALL ITS BEAUTY PURPOSES

Coconut oil? The thing you fry eggs in? Cook chicken in? You're now telling me I can use it as a beauty product?! Yes, I know I sound as though I'm going mad but the great news is, I'm not. Coconut oil is made up of 48% lauric acid (one of the only other places you'll find this is in mother's breast milk). It is full of health-boosting and skin-loving properties because it is antibacterial and antifungal. It's also high in vitamin E.

We've also written a beauty book called *Natural Beauty with Coconut Oil*, which is full of at-home beauty recipes. But for now, here are some of the ways you can use Lucy Bee coconut oil as a beauty product:

✦ **Moisturizer.** Apply all over, but remember, a little goes a long way!

✦ **Make-up remover.** Yes, even waterproof mascara. Using less than a pea-sized amount, warm the coconut oil in your fingertips and apply to the lashes. Then wipe away using a damp cotton wool pad.

✦ **Hair Mask.** Once a week apply from the roots to the end of the hair, massaging it in, then leave it for as long as possible. Wash out with two shampoos and one conditioner.

✦ **Massage oil.** Warm up before applying in your hands.

✦ **Oil pulling.** This is an ancient Ayurvedic treatment to help remove toxins from the body. Using a teaspoon or tablespoon of coconut oil, swish around your mouth like mouthwash from anywhere between five

to 20 minutes. Then spit it out in the bin (not the sink as it will block the drains when it solidifies).

✦ **Body scrub.** Using coconut oil and one of our bath salts, mix equal amounts of both and apply to your skin. You can even add essential oils too.

✦ **Deodorant.** Apply a thin layer to your underarms.

✦ **Toothpaste.** Mix equal amounts of bicarbonate of soda and coconut oil and scrub those pearly whites!

✦ **Cuticle oil.** Massage a small amount onto your cuticle beds and leave to soak in.

✦ **Deep hand and foot treatment.** Apply coconut oil over your hands or feet, then wrap in cling film. Leave for as long as possible.

We humans aren't the only ones who can't get enough of coconut oil... animals love it too! We are often sent photos of dogs, cats, geckos, horses, ducks, chickens and tortoises getting their daily fix of coconut oil.

I love seeing your photos on our social media so please do carry on sending them in to us. I'm really looking forward to hearing what you think of the book and which recipes are your favourites. If you don't already, why not follow us on social media so I can see your creations and hear your thoughts.

Feel free to experiment and play around with the recipes to suit your own taste and, above all, enjoy them. I recently read that rather than thinking of cooking as a chore, use it as an excuse for a little 'me time'. I love putting on some music (sometimes with a glass of wine to hand) and creating my own little masterpieces!

Thank you so much for your support!

Love,
Lucy Bee x

STORECUPBOARD STAPLES & ESSENTIAL EQUIPMENT

We all have our own favourites, those go-to ingredients that we can't be without and use so often in numerous recipes, and the following are mine – ready for making simple, nutritious meals. At home, we always make everything from scratch, whether it's our own sauces, stocks or even curry powders, so I've tried to include the basics for these here, too, as they can really transform your meals.

   As well as fully-stocked kitchen cupboards, a range of equipment makes preparing food easier.

✦ **Lucy Bee coconut oil.** This should be your go-to cooking oil. If you need to soften it to use in cooking or baking, then either melt it in the oven as it preheats, or place the jar in warm water, on a radiator, Aga, or even briefly in the microwave.

✦ **Apple cider vinegar.** I love the raw, organic, unfiltered and undistilled cloudy version, which still has the 'mother of vinegar', or cloudy sediment, that contains most of the health-promoting bacterial properties.

✦ **Eggs.** Organic, free-range eggs are worth the extra cost, as you know what the chickens have been fed, meaning it's all free from chemicals. I hate the idea of battery hens too, so I always buy organic chicken, and would rather go without if I can't find organic.

✦ **Green tea.** I always have a cafetière on the go, full of green tea.

✦ **Healthy oils.** As well as my Lucy Bee, I keep a bottle of Udo's oil in the cupboard for endless body-loving benefits.

✦ **Herbs.** I love how you can transform a recipe simply by adding some herbs to the dish. Generally, the longer these are left to work their magic the better.

✦ **Lucy Bee cacao powder.** While you can use unsweetened cocoa powder in recipes, cacao is much better for you as it retains all its nutrients and wonderful antioxidants. It can even send moods soaring. What's not to like?

✦ **Lucy Bee cinnamon powder.** This natural sweetener is a traditional remedy for digestive problems and tastes really great when added to your porridge.

✦ **Lucy Bee Himalayan salt.** Not all salts are equal! This pretty pink salt helps to balance the body's pH levels, as well as aiding nutrient absorption.

✦ **Lucy Bee lucuma powder.** A natural sweetener from Peru that works a treat in baking recipes.

✦ **Lucy Bee maca powder.** This superfood is a great energy boost and hormone regulator and I use it often in my smoothies.

✦ **Lucy Bee turmeric powder.** Not only does this add an amazing depth of colour to foods but it brings with it lots of natural anti-inflammatory properties. I love sprinkling it over fried eggs and stirring it into vegetables.

✦ **Nuts.** Brazils, cashews, walnuts, pecans and almonds are all brilliantly healthy and versatile. Their oils are especially beneficial.

✦ **Seeds.** I use all sorts of seeds, from pumpkin to sunflower and chia. Try sprouting alfalfa seeds, so easy to do and wonderfully healthy. They make a lovely topping for dishes or filling in sandwiches.

✦ **Spices.** Keep a range, ideally buying them whole and then grinding them yourself in a nut and seed or even coffee grinder, for fresher and cheaper blends. If you make too much of any spice mixes, store them in your empty Lucy Bee jars.

✦ **Stocks.** At home we always make our own stocks (check out the recipes on pages 176 and 177) as they're great to add to soups, risottos etc. and you can also limit the amount of salt in them.

✦ **Sugar alternatives.** I love lucuma powder, maple syrup, manuka honey and coconut sugar, and use them in recipes and baking in place of processed sugars.

✦ **Xanthan gum.** Wonderful for gluten-free cooking.

ESSENTIAL EQUIPMENT
Everyone has their own favourite kitchen gadgets – my must-haves include:

✦ **Blender**

✦ **Spiralizer.** This handy gadget turns vegetables into long, fine strands that can be eaten in place of pasta, as in my 'courgetti' recipe on page 89.

✦ **Thermometer or Thermapen.** Great for checking if meat is cooked.

✦ **Seed and nut blitzer (or coffee grinder)**

✦ **Cafetière**, for green tea.

✦ **Digital scales**, for easy, accurate measurements, especially of very small quantities.

✦ **Food processor**

✦ **Garlic slicer.** Whilst not completely essential, this handy gadget saves time and effort, plus it means your hands don't end up smelling overwhelmingly of garlic. Bonus!

✦ **Juicer**

✦ **Good-quality spring-form cake tins**, to make it even easier to remove your favourite cakes from the tins.

✦ **Heavy-based saucepans.** If possible, it's really worth investing in these as the heat is evenly distributed.

✦ **Sharp knives.** This might sound obvious, but it really makes a difference in having a selection of sharp knives to make the chopping and slicing of ingredients so much easier.

✦ **Steamer.** Steaming retains all the nutrients in vegetables, but if you don't have a steamer, place the vegetables inside a metal colander, pop this on top of a large saucepan or pot, fill the pan with just enough water so that the colander isn't touching it, then bring to a gentle simmer and cover.

✦ **Tefal Infiny Force hand-held blender.** I love this for making homemade mayonnaise – it's really quick and simple to use.

BRUNCHIN'

We've been programmed to think
that you have to have things like
cereal for breakfast but this really
isn't the case. I want to turn your
idea of breakfast on its head
by showing you that you don't
always have to have your typical
yoghurt and granola, or cereal and
milk combination. This is a great
opportunity to get in some greens
and start your day the right way.
Some of our recipes here bring a
bit of spice, like our chorizo wraps.
Or how about our scrambled tofu to
bring a twist to a typical scrambled
egg? And of course, how could we
have a book without waffles? These
are perfect for the weekends and
go hand-in-hand with a green tea
or coffee.

JUICES

You are guaranteed to feel good after drinking the rainbow! These are a great way to pack in those nutrients in one drink and are ideal to take out with you on the go. Remember to use your recycled Lucy Bee jars, they're great for your juices, smoothies and snacks!

RAINBOW JUICE

SERVES 1
2 carrots
Handful of spinach
Slice–½ lemon, to taste
1 apple
1 beetroot (beet)

Wash all the ingredients and peel the beetroot (beet). Put into a juicer and serve with ice.

GREEN JUICE

SERVES 1
1 celery stick
½ cucumber
Handful of spinach
¼ pineapple, peeled
2.5cm/1in piece of fresh ginger

Wash all ingredients, then put into a juicer and serve with ice.

GF WF LF DF V VEG   GF WF LF DF V VEG

SMOOTHIES

Mixing and matching smoothie ingredients is a perfect way to add variety to your drinks. These are two of our favourites here at Lucy Bee. The ideal way to disguise those good greens for those who aren't keen on eating them.

BANANA AND ALMOND BUTTER SMOOTHIE

SERVES 1
1 banana
1 tbsp almond butter
200ml/¾ cup plus 1 tbsp
   almond milk
½ tsp Lucy Bee cinnamon powder
   (optional)

Add all ingredients to a blender and blitz until smooth, then serve straight away.

CARDAMOM MANGO BLISS

SERVES 1
100g/3½ oz mango
Seeds from 1 cardamom pod
Handful of spinach
½ avocado
200ml/¾ cup plus 1 tbsp coconut
   water or water

Add all ingredients to a blender and blitz until smooth, then serve straight away.

TIP
For an iced option to enjoy on warm sunny days, freeze the banana first.

GF   WF   LF   DF   V   VEG   GF   WF   LF   DF   V   VEG

SPICED APPLE AND CRANBERRY PORRIDGE

Porridge has been around forever and will never become boring when you can so easily adapt the toppings to suit your mood. This recipe really spices it up, making it very warming, especially in the winter months.

Put the oats and almond milk in a saucepan and gently bring to the boil, stirring. Once it bubbles and the oats have absorbed the liquid, add the mixed spice, lucuma and vanilla seeds and pod, if using. Remove the pan from the heat and leave to rest for 3–4 minutes.

While the oats are resting, melt the coconut oil in a frying pan, add the apple slices and cinnamon and sauté until the apple is soft, then add the cranberries.

Remove the vanilla pod from the porridge and serve topped with the apple and cranberries. For extra flavour, add an extra sprinkling of cinnamon.

40g/scant ½ cup gluten-free oats
200ml/¾ cup plus 1 tbsp
    almond milk
½ tsp mixed spice
1 tsp Lucy Bee lucuma powder
½ vanilla pod, split lengthways and
    seeds scraped out (optional)
1 tbsp Lucy Bee coconut oil
1 apple, thinly sliced
1 tsp Lucy Bee cinnamon powder,
    plus extra to serve
40g/½ cup dried cranberries

SERVES 2

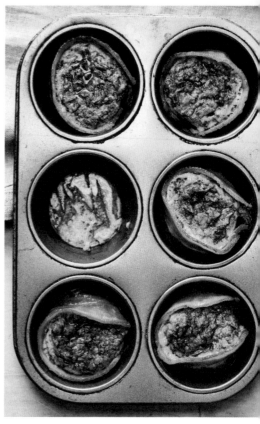

EGGS IN BLANKETS WITH CORIANDER

This is our take on the traditional 'pigs in blankets'.
These little muffins are surprisingly easy to make.

Preheat the oven to 180°C/350°F/gas mark 4. Grease
9 cups of a deep cupcake tray with the coconut oil.

Stick one slice of bacon onto the inside of each cup.
Crack the eggs into a mixing jug and add the coriander
(cilantro) and some seasoning. Whisk well and pour into
each cup, to come around halfway up each one.

Bake in the oven for 16–18 minutes, or until a knife
inserted into the middle of one of the muffins comes
out dry.

1 tsp Lucy Bee coconut oil
9 slices of streaky bacon
6 medium eggs
30g/1oz fresh coriander (cilantro),
    chopped
Pinch of Lucy Bee Himalayan salt
    and ground black pepper

MAKES 9

SCRAMBLED TOFU

Simple, nutritious and satisfying. Scramble up
some tofu whenever you fancy a change from eggs!

Melt the coconut oil in a non-stick pan then add
the garlic and chilli and sauté for 1 minute over a
medium heat. Add the tomatoes, spring onions
(scallions), mushrooms, peas and turmeric and
cook for a further 3–4 minutes.

Add the tofu (beancurd), reduce the heat and
cook for a further 3–4 minutes. Add salt and pepper
to taste and serve hot, with the sliced avocado on top.

1 tbsp Lucy Bee coconut oil
2 garlic cloves, finely chopped
½ red chilli, finely chopped
2 medium tomatoes, quartered
2 spring onions (scallions), chopped
50g/1 cup button mushrooms,
    quartered
20g/¾ oz frozen peas
½ tsp Lucy Bee turmeric powder
200g/7 oz tofu (beancurd), crumbled
    into small pieces
Lucy Bee Himalayan salt and ground
    black pepper
1 avocado, sliced, to serve

SERVES 2

MOROCCAN EGGS

The mere thought of this delicious dish makes me feel hungry! It really is comfort food at its best and works well at any time of the day. I enjoy having it for breakfast, lunch or dinner.

Melt the coconut oil in a deep frying pan over a medium heat. Add the onion and garlic and cook until golden, then add the harissa paste and ground coriander and stir well for 1 minute.

Add the stock and chickpeas (garbanzo beans) then cover the pan and turn down the heat slightly. Simmer for 10 minutes, adding extra stock if you think it needs it. Using a potato masher, gently squash the chickpeas so that the sauce thickens but remains chunky. Add the tomatoes, courgette (zucchini), pepper and spinach and season generously. Stir well and cook for 10 minutes. Once the juice has begun to reduce, make 4 indents in the mixture and crack an egg into each. Cover the pan and cook for the last 5 minutes, until the eggs are set. Season to taste and serve, sprinkled with fresh coriander (cilantro).

1 tbsp Lucy Bee coconut oil
1 red onion, finely chopped
3 garlic cloves, finely diced
½ tbsp harissa paste
½ tsp ground coriander
300ml/1¼ cups vegetable stock (see page 176 for homemade)
240g/1¾ cups chickpeas (garbanzo beans), drained weight
1 x 400g tin/2 cups chopped tomatoes
1 courgette (zucchini), quartered lengthways and sliced
1 red pepper (bell pepper), deseeded and sliced
140g/5oz spinach
4 eggs
Lucy Bee Himalayan salt and ground black pepper
Coriander (cilantro) sprigs, to serve

SERVES 4

WAFFLES

As our social media followers will know, we have a serious love of pancakes so it only made sense to adapt the recipe for our 'old favourite' into waffles. Choose your own toppings as you would in a 'pick-and-mix' and serve with your most loved ingredients.

In a large bowl, mix together the buckwheat flour, rice flour and baking powder. Separate the eggs, placing the whites in one bowl and the yolks in another.

Add the almond milk and melted coconut oil to the egg yolks. Beat together using an electric whisk. Beat the milk and egg yolk mixture into the flour mixture.

Using a clean electric whisk, beat the egg whites until stiff peaks form, then gently fold the egg whites into the milk, egg and flour mixture.

Add a small amount of coconut oil to both sides (top and bottom) of your waffle maker or waffle iron, and cook as per the instructions for your machine. Serve with maple syrup and other toppings of your choice.

100g/1 scant cup buckwheat flour
100g/¾ cup rice flour
2 tsp gluten-free baking powder
2 eggs
400ml/1½ cups plus 2 tbsp
    almond milk
50ml/scant ¼ cup melted Lucy Bee
    coconut oil, plus extra for cooking
Maple syrup, to serve

MAKES 10 WAFFLES

TIP
These waffles freeze brilliantly and are great for a quick healthy snack. This batter can also be used to make pancakes.

GF WF LF DF V VEG

HEALTHY, SUPERFOOD QUINOA BARS

When you crave something sweet but want to be healthy, these bars are the best snack to make. They're not too sweet and you can really taste the contrast in flavours. These are best stored in the freezer but I'd recommend taking them out a few minutes before eating so that they soften up slightly.

Cook the quinoa according to the instructions on the packet and leave to cool. Put into a large bowl with all the other ingredients and mix well until evenly combined.

Line a small baking tray with baking parchment and spread the mixture out evenly. Chill in the fridge for at least 2 hours before cutting into bars. Store in the freezer.

60g/⅓ cup quinoa
100g/1 cup gluten-free oats
100g/¾ cup hazelnuts, chopped
½ tsp Lucy Bee Himalayan salt
1 tsp Lucy Bee maca powder
1 tsp Lucy Bee cinnamon powder
100g/3½ oz dried cranberries
3 tbsp honey
40g/1½ oz dark chocolate (at least 70% cocoa solids), finely chopped
65g/2¼ oz Lucy Bee coconut oil, melted

MAKES 12–15

STUFFED TOMATOES

As appealing to the eye as they are to the taste buds. Quick and simple to make, these are perfect for a side dish with fish or can be served on their own for a lighter meal.

Preheat the oven to 180°C/350°F/gas mark 4.

Toast the pine nuts in a dry frying pan for 1–2 minutes, tossing frequently to prevent them from burning. Tip into a small mixing bowl.

Add the olives, oregano, feta and breadcrumbs to the pine nuts, season and stir well to mix. Spoon the mixture evenly into the scooped out tomato halves, place on a baking tray and bake in the oven for 20–30 minutes, until nicely browned on top and the tomatoes are cooked.

Leave to cool slightly, top with some chopped parsley and serve.

20g/¾ oz pine nuts
8 pitted black olives, quartered
1 tbsp fresh oregano leaves, finely
  chopped
80g/2¾ oz feta, crumbled
1 slice of gluten-free bread, blitzed
  to breadcrumbs
4 large beef tomatoes, halved and
  insides scooped out
Lucy Bee Himalayan salt and ground
  black pepper
Chopped parsley, to serve

SERVES 2–4

BREAKFAST BURGERS

Start your day the right way by getting in four vegetables that you might not normally think to include in your breakfast. Eating healthily never tasted so good.

Preheat the oven to 180°C/350°F/gas mark 4.

Wrap the grated courgette (zucchini) in several sheets of kitchen paper or a clean tea towel and press down firmly to squeeze out the water. Add to a mixing bowl with the leek, chilli, cauliflower 'rice', rice flour and beaten egg. Season and stir well. Roll into 2 evenly sized balls.

Place the tomato slices on a baking tray and top each with a slice of goat's cheese. Bake in the oven for 8 minutes, until nicely melting.

Meanwhile, melt the coconut oil in a frying pan over a high heat and, when hot, place both burgers in the pan and press firmly down to make a burger-shaped fritter. Cook for 2 minutes on each side over a high heat then reduce the heat and cook for a further 2 minutes on each side, or until cooked through, being careful not to burn them.

To assemble, place a tomato and goat's cheese stack on top of each burger, add a grinding of pepper and a couple of parsley leaves to each and serve.

150g/5¼ oz courgette (zucchini), grated
150g/5¼ oz leek, diced
½ green chilli, chopped
3 cauliflower florets, blitzed in a food processor to make 'rice'
40g/⅓ cup rice flour
1 egg, beaten
2 slices of tomato
2 slices of goat's cheese
1 tbsp Lucy Bee coconut oil
Lucy Bee Himalayan salt and ground black pepper
Few parsley leaves, to serve

SERVES 2

TIP
Use up any leftover vegetables that you have in the fridge by substituting (or adding to) our suggestions.

CHORIZO WRAP

Transform your table into your very own tapas bar.
Our Spanish twist on a flavoursome, filling wrap is
sure to delight.

Melt the coconut oil in a deep frying pan. Add the
potato and cook over a high heat for 5 minutes or until
golden at the edges, then add the chorizo and cook for
a further 5 minutes over a medium heat.

Add the (bell) pepper, onion, tomatoes, paprika and
some seasoning to taste. Cook for 5 minutes over a
medium heat then turn the heat to low, cover and
cook for 30 minutes or until all the ingredients are soft.

Meanwhile, mix together the yoghurt, lime zest
and juice.

Divide the chorizo mixture evenly between the
wraps and top with the yoghurt mixture, parsley and
avocado slices.

1 tbsp Lucy Bee coconut oil
180g/6¼ oz potato, peeled and cut
   into 5mm/⅕ in dice
50g/1¾ oz chorizo, finely chopped
1 yellow pepper (bell pepper),
   deseeded and sliced
1 red onion, chopped
2 medium tomatoes, chopped
1 tsp hot paprika
Lucy Bee Himalayan salt and ground
   black pepper

TO SERVE
2 tbsp Greek yoghurt
Finely grated zest and juice of ½ lime
2 gluten-free tortilla wraps
Chopped fresh parsley
1 avocado, sliced

SERVES 2

TIP
Great food for socializing — put
everything on the table and let
people help themselves.

SPICY BEAN BURGERS

For those days when you want to avoid meat, this burger is the one for you. These make a nutritious lunch, light dinner or even breakfast, and can also be eaten cold. 'Meat-free Mondays' have never been so easy!

Melt 1 tsp of the coconut oil in a frying pan over a medium heat, add the garlic and onion and sauté until golden. Add the cumin seeds, chilli and cayenne pepper, and stir. Continue to cook over a medium to low heat for a few minutes to allow the spices to be absorbed, then transfer to a bowl and add the spinach, beans, breadcrumbs and some seasoning. Using your hands, combine and shape into 2 burgers.

Add the remaining coconut oil to the frying pan and, when hot, add the burgers. Cook for 4–6 minutes on each side over a medium heat, until cooked through and a golden colour. They are quite delicate, so be careful when cooking.

Serve with your favourite toppings, with a salad or with roasted broccoli and garlic.

2 tbsp Lucy Bee coconut oil
2 garlic cloves, finely chopped
1 red onion, finely chopped
1 tsp cumin seeds
1 small to medium red chilli, finely sliced
½ tsp cayenne pepper
Handful of spinach, roughly chopped
1 x 400g tin/1⅓ cups cannellini beans, drained weight
60g/1 generous cup gluten-free breadcrumbs
Lucy Bee Himalayan salt and ground black pepper

SERVES 2

PRAWN BURGERS

These burgers are really popular in a restaurant I go to in Florida with the family, but sadly I usually can't join in on the fun of eating them. However, now I can – we experimented and made some Lucy Bee style! Served with our healthy marie rose sauce, these are the perfect duo.

Preheat the oven to 180°C/350°F/gas mark 4. Divide the prawns (shrimp) into 2 equal portions.

Add one portion to a food processor with the breadcrumbs, parsley and some salt and pepper, blitz together then place in a mixing bowl.

Chop the remaining prawns into about 4, depending on their size, and add to the mixing bowl, along with the egg. Using your hands, combine well then divide the mixture into 2 even-sized burgers. Dust with gluten-free flour on each side.

Heat an ovenproof frying pan over a medium heat and add the coconut oil. Once hot, place both burgers in the pan and fry for 2 minutes on each side to seal. Transfer the pan to the oven for about 10 minutes, until cooked through.

Meanwhile, to make the sauce, stir together all the ingredients in a bowl.

Place each burger on a bed of rocket (arugula) and top with a slice of tomato. Serve with the marie rose sauce and a lemon wedge.

180g/6¼ oz raw jumbo or king prawns (shrimp), peeled and deveined
80g/1½ cups gluten-free breadcrumbs
20g/¾ oz fresh parsley
1 egg
Gluten-free flour, for dusting
1 tbsp Lucy Bee coconut oil
Lucy Bee Himalayan salt and ground black pepper

FOR THE MARIE ROSE SAUCE
1 tsp tomato purée (paste)
1 tbsp Greek yoghurt
Finely grated zest and juice of ¼ lemon
1 tsp balsamic vinegar

TO SERVE
Rocket (arugula)
Sliced tomato
Lemon wedges

SERVES 2

HASH BROWNS WITH SALMON AND LUCY BEE TARTAR SAUCE

I love adding a healthy twist to old favourites so using sweet potatoes for hash browns really fits the bill here. Cashews are a wonderful way to thicken a sauce and add a creamy texture.

Peel the sweet potatoes and grate them on a coarse setting, then wrap in a kitchen towel and squeeze to remove the moisture. Add to a mixing bowl with the feta, eggs and some salt and pepper. Using your hands, mix everything together then split the mixture evenly in half (or in quarters if you would prefer smaller hash browns). Roll each into a ball and flatten into a hash brown shape.

Heat the coconut oil in a frying pan and, when hot, add the hash browns and fry over a medium heat for about 4 minutes on each side, or until evenly cooked (I like them slightly crispy, but reduce the heat if they start to cook too quickly on the outside).

Meanwhile, to make the tartar sauce, blitz the ingredients together in a food processor until the sauce has the required consistency, adding a splash of water to loosen if needed.

To serve, top the hash browns with smoked salmon and watercress and finish with the tartar sauce.

2 medium-sized sweet potatoes
35g/1¼ oz feta, crumbled
2 eggs
1 tbsp Lucy Bee coconut oil
50g/1¾ oz smoked salmon
20g/¾ oz watercress
Lucy Bee Himalayan salt and ground black pepper

FOR THE TARTAR SAUCE

30g/1oz cashew nuts, soaked in boiling water for 10 minutes to soften, then drained
Finely grated zest and juice of ½ lemon
½ tbsp capers
1 tbsp Greek yoghurt
½ tsp extra virgin olive oil

SERVES 2

SUMMER PASTA SALAD

Cook the pasta according to the instructions on the packet, rinse in cold water and drain. Add to a mixing or serving bowl and mix in the sun-dried tomato oil.

Melt the coconut oil in a frying pan, add the aubergine (eggplant) cubes and sauté until tender, adding more oil if needed (aubergines love oil). Stir into the pasta, along with the remaining ingredients, including salt and pepper to taste and a squeeze of lemon juice. Give it a good stir and serve immediately. It's also good the next day for a speedy lunch.

200g/7oz brown rice pasta
75g/⅔ cup sun-dried tomatoes in oil, chopped, plus 4 tbsp of the oil
1 tbsp Lucy Bee coconut oil
1 aubergine (eggplant), about 200g/ 7 oz, cut into small cubes
75g/¾ cup pitted olives, sliced
75g/½ cup pumpkin seeds or pine nuts, toasted in a dry pan
100g/3½ oz goat's cheese, cubed
Handful mix of basil, coriander (cilantro) and parsley, chopped
6 spring onions (scallions), sliced
100g/3½ oz rocket (arugula)
Juice of ½ lemon
Lucy Bee Himalayan salt and ground black pepper

SERVES 2–4

TIP
I use Rizopia brown rice pasta.

BROCCOLI AND LEMON PASTA

Preheat the oven to 180°C/350°F/gas mark 4.

Melt the coconut oil in a wide, heavy-based ovenproof frying pan. When hot, add the garlic, lemon (giving it a squeeze to release some of the juice), broccoli, thyme and some salt and pepper. Stir everything together then place the pan in the oven for 15 minutes.

Meanwhile, cook the pasta according to the packet instructions, then drain and rinse under cold water to stop it cooking further.

Take the pan out of the oven, remove the broccoli to a plate and place the pan over a medium-high heat. Add the wine and allow it to bubble a little then reduce to a syrupy consistency. Remove the fresh thyme, if using, stir in the pasta and heat it through quickly, stirring. Add the broccoli, check the seasoning and serve.

1 tbsp Lucy Bee coconut oil
2 garlic cloves, crushed
1 lemon, quartered
200g/7oz long-stemmed broccoli
½ tsp dried thyme or few sprigs of fresh thyme
150g/5¼ oz brown rice pasta (I use Rizopia brand)
100ml/scant ½ cup dry white wine
Lucy Bee Himalayan salt and ground black pepper

SERVES 2

GLOW WITH
THE FLOW

To me the word 'glow' beams with
health and wellbeing. The recipes
in this chapter are nutritious, filling,
refreshing and full of skin- and body-
loving ingredients. You'll find these
recipes are based on lots of vegetables
and sometimes fish too. You'll soon be
glowing top to toe with the following:
Thai Mango Salad, Mackerel Muffins
or Pea, Mint and Asparagus Risotto.

THAI MANGO SALAD

Your taste buds will thank you for this one! From the red onion, to the peanut butter, to the fresh mango, this very light and satisfying Thai salad can be enjoyed all year round – especially since the two seasons for mangos overlap, perfect!

Heat the coconut oil in a wok or deep non-stick frying pan, add the onion and cook until soft, then add the red and white cabbage and fry for a further 5 minutes.

Add the bean sprouts, edamame beans, carrot, sesame oil, tamari and peanut butter. Stir well over a medium heat for about 8–10 minutes, until the ingredients are soft and combined.

Top with the mango and peanuts and serve with a wedge of lime.

1 tbsp Lucy Bee coconut oil
1 large red onion, sliced
50g/1¾ oz mixture of red and white cabbage, sliced
100g/1¾ cups bean sprouts
100g/¾ cup edamame beans
1 large carrot, grated
1 tbsp sesame oil
1½ tbsp tamari sauce
1 tbsp peanut butter (crunchy or smooth)
30g/1 oz mango, diced
Handful of peanuts
Lime wedges, to serve

SERVES 2

TIP
This dish works really well with chicken and prawns (shrimp) added too.

TUNA AND CANNELLINI BEAN NIÇOISE

For all those 'ladies who lunch', here's our very own twist on an old favourite. Keep it clean with our homemade dressing. (Oh and feel free to share with the men in your life too.)

To make the dressing, place all the ingredients into a protein shaker and shake to mix together, or use a small balloon whisk and bowl.

Cook the eggs in a pan of boiling water for 8 minutes, then drain and run under cold water, until cold. Peel and cut each into quarters.

If using fresh tuna, heat the coconut oil in a griddle pan or frying pan over a medium heat. When hot, add the tuna steak and cook for 3 minutes, then turn over and cook for a further 3 minutes, depending on the thickness of the steak. Remove from the heat and, if you like your tuna rare, move onto a plate (leave it in the pan if you prefer it cooked through).

Mix the onion, tomatoes, cucumber, lettuce and cannellini beans together and divide between 2 bowls. Flake the tuna over the salad and top with the egg quarters, placing an anchovy fillet over each. Scatter over the olives and drizzle with the dressing to serve.

2 eggs, at room temperature
200g/7oz fresh tuna steak or 200g/7 oz canned tuna in spring water, drained
1 tsp Lucy Bee coconut oil (if using fresh tuna)
1 red onion, finely sliced
100g/3½ oz tomatoes (choose the best available), halved or quartered
¼ cucumber, peeled, deseeded and cut into chunks
½ romaine lettuce, thinly sliced
1 x 400g tin/1⅓ cups cannellini beans, drained and rinsed
8 anchovy fillets in oil
Handful of green or black olives

FOR THE DRESSING
100ml/scant ½ cup extra virgin olive oil
50ml/scant ¼ cup apple cider vinegar
1 tsp Dijon mustard
1 tsp honey
1 garlic clove, finely chopped
Lucy Bee Himalayan salt and ground black pepper, to taste

SERVES 2

BUTTERNUT SQUASH AND GOAT'S CHEESE SALAD

For me, goat's cheese is one of those ingredients which really transforms a dish. I add it to even the simplest of recipes for that little added extra. With its variety of colour and texture this salad is as appealing to look at as it is to eat.

Preheat the oven to 180°C/350°F/gas mark 4.

Mix the butternut squash with the melted coconut oil and nigella seeds. Spread out on a baking tray and cook for 30–40 minutes until soft, turning occasionally.

Meanwhile, make the dressing by mixing together all the ingredients, with salt and pepper to taste; I use a protein blender bottle to do this.

Place the kale or cavolo nero and red onion in a mixing bowl and pour over the dressing. Toss to mix and set aside for 30–40 minutes, to allow the vegetables to soften and absorb the flavours of the dressing.

Cook the green beans in a pan of boiling water for 3–5 minutes, until cooked to your liking, then drain and rinse in cold water.

Transfer the kale or cavolo nero and red onion to a salad bowl, add the green beans, pumpkin seeds, goat's cheese and butternut squash, and serve.

600g/1lb 5oz butternut squash, deseeded, peeled and cut into 2cm/¾ in cubes
20g/¾ oz Lucy Bee coconut oil, melted
1 tbsp nigella seeds
100g/3½ oz kale, cavolo nero or any dark green cabbage, finely sliced
180g/6¼ oz red onions, thinly sliced
100g/3½ oz green beans, chopped
30g/¼ cup pumpkin seeds, toasted in a dry pan
50g/1¾ oz goat's cheese, sliced

FOR THE DRESSING
1–2 tbsp Dijon mustard, to taste
1–2 garlic cloves, crushed or finely chopped
2 tbsp apple cider vinegar
90ml/¼ cup plus 2 tbsp extra virgin olive oil
50ml/scant ¼ cup maple syrup
Lucy Bee Himalayan salt and ground black pepper

SERVES 2–4

THE ULTIMATE SALAD

This works equally well as a meal on its own or as a side with most meats. I usually have it with lamb kebabs or chicken. Feel free to experiment and add in any of your own must-have ingredients.

Cook the quinoa according to the packet instructions. Put the onion in a small bowl, add the lime juice and set aside to marinate for 1 hour.

Put all the other ingredients in a large mixing bowl, add the marinated onion, stir together and season. Serve with a wedge of lemon and a side bowl of corn chips.

100g/½ cup plus 1½ tbsp quinoa
1 medium red onion, chopped
Juice of 1 lime
140g/5 oz cherry tomatoes, halved
80g/⅔ cup mixed olives, pitted
120g/4¼ oz roasted red peppers (from a jar), diced
Handful of coriander (cilantro), finely chopped
150g/1 cup tinned black (turtle) beans, drained weight
100g/¾ cup tinned chickpeas (garbanzo beans), drained weight
50g/scant 1 cup sun-dried tomatoes from a jar, chopped, and 1 tbsp of the oil
50g/1¾ oz feta, diced
30g/1oz jalapeños from a jar, sliced
1 tbsp extra virgin olive oil
Lucy Bee Himalayan salt and ground black pepper

TO SERVE
Lemon wedges
75g/2½ oz corn chips

SERVES 2

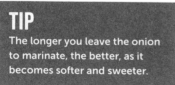

TIP
The longer you leave the onion to marinate, the better, as it becomes softer and sweeter.

GF WF LF DF V VEG

PEA, MINT AND ASPARAGUS RISOTTO

A lighter version of a dish I like to eat in restaurants. The trick here is to give the rice time to swell and absorb the stock, so taking in all that goodness. You can enjoy this either hot or cold.

Melt the coconut oil in a large pan, stir in the risotto rice to coat in the oil, then add the stock and simmer over a medium heat for 15 minutes, stirring continuously, until the risotto rice has softened and turned plump (as it has mostly absorbed the stock).

Add the peas, asparagus, mint and salt and pepper to taste. Continue to cook for a further 5 minutes or until the stock has been completely absorbed, the rice is just tender and the risotto has a thick, creamy texture.

30g Lucy Bee coconut oil
225g/1¼ cups risotto rice
1 litre/4 cups vegetable stock
   (see page 176 for homemade)
300g/2½ cups frozen peas
100g/3½ cups asparagus, ends
   removed and spears halved
1 tbsp mint leaves, chopped
Lucy Bee Himalayan salt and ground
   black pepper

SERVES 2

MACKEREL MUFFINS

A wonderful way to boost your omega-3 intake,
these muffins work well as a snack on the go. These
are great served with asparagus – I was interested to
learn that asparagus was one of the reasons food lovers
discovered a fifth taste, umami, as it's neither sweet,
sour, salty or bitter.

Preheat the oven to 180°C/350°F/gas mark 4.

Add ½ tsp coconut oil to each of 4 muffin holes in a
muffin tray, then place into the oven for 5 minutes to
heat while you make the mixture.

Put the eggs, flour, baking powder, milk, parsley, chives
and some salt and pepper into a large mixing bowl and,
using an electric whisk, mix together until thick and
smooth. Add the shredded mackerel and stir to combine,
using a spoon.

Remove the muffin tray from the oven and spoon the
mixture evenly into the 4 oiled cases of the tray, taking
care as the oil will be very hot.

Bake in the oven for 15 minutes until cooked through
and springy to the touch. Remove from the oven and
turn out onto a wire rack. These can be served hot
or cold and are good with horseradish sauce or our
homemade Tartar Sauce (see page 43).

2 tsp Lucy Bee coconut oil
2 eggs
100g/¾ cup gluten-free
    self-raising flour
1 tsp gluten-free baking powder
3 tbsp milk
5g/⅛ oz fresh parsley, finely
    chopped
5g/⅛ oz fresh chives, finely chopped
Lucy Bee Himalayan salt and ground
    black pepper
1 smoked mackerel fillet, shredded

SERVES 4

CRUSHED SMOKED MACKEREL FISH CAKES

Fish cakes are one of those things that I can never eat in restaurants, which is why I wanted to share this recipe. If you have any left over, they work well served with an egg for breakfast.

Add the potatoes and ginger to a pan of cold water and bring to the boil. Turn the heat down and simmer until cooked, then drain, remove the ginger and allow the potatoes to cool a little before crushing (I use my hands for this, wearing latex gloves, as it gives the fish cakes a nice texture).

While the potatoes are cooking, remove the skin and any bones from the mackerel and flake into pieces. Put into a mixing bowl with the capers and spring onions (scallions). Add the crushed potatoes to the fish mixture and combine well, adding salt and pepper to taste.

Break the mixture into 6 portions and flatten each slightly, then dip each one in breadcrumbs to coat. Heat the coconut oil in a non-stick frying pan over a medium heat and, when hot, add the fish cakes and cook for 3 minutes on each side (you may need to add a little more oil).

300g/10½ oz potatoes, peeled and quartered
2 slices of peeled fresh ginger
250g/8¾ oz peppered smoked mackerel
30g/1 oz capers, chopped
6 spring onions (scallions), finely chopped
100g/2 cups gluten-free breadcrumbs
Lucy Bee Himalayan salt and ground black pepper
30g/1 oz Lucy Bee coconut oil

MAKES 6

SEA BASS WITH MEDITERRANEAN CRUSHED POTATOES

My twist for a 'fish on Friday' dinner. An easy dish that your family and friends are sure to be impressed with.

Boil the potatoes with a pinch of salt in a saucepan until tender, then drain and set aside. Melt 1 tbsp of the coconut oil in a deep frying pan over a medium heat, add both (bell) peppers and cook for 3–5 minutes, until just starting to soften. Add the drained potatoes, the capers and olives, and season generously.

Remove the pan from the heat, add the olive oil and, using a potato masher, lightly crush the potatoes and mix the ingredients together.

Transfer the potato mixture to a dish and keep warm. Place the frying pan back over a medium heat and add the remaining 1 tbsp coconut oil, then the garlic and lemon zest and juice. Sizzle for a minute, then add the sea bass fillets skin side up and then the samphire. Fry for 2 minutes then turn the fish over to cook skin side down for a further 4–6 minutes. Check the fish is cooked through before removing from the heat. Remove the fish from the pan and keep warm.

Add a little coconut oil to the pan and quickly fry the chilli, spring onions (scallions) and parsley. Spoon the potato mixture onto 2 plates and place the sea bass on top. Spoon the chilli, spring onion and parsley mixture over the fish and serve with lemon wedges.

400g/14 oz new potatoes, quartered
2 tbsp Lucy Bee coconut oil
1 red pepper (bell pepper), deseeded and diced
1 green pepper (bell pepper), deseeded and diced
1 tbsp capers
50g/½ cup pitted mixed olives, halved
2 tbsp extra virgin olive oil
2 garlic cloves, finely chopped
Finely grated zest and juice of ½ lemon
2 sea bass fillets
1 tbsp fresh samphire
1 red chilli, finely sliced
2 spring onions (scallions), finely sliced
Big handful of parsley, roughly chopped
Lucy Bee Himalayan salt and ground black pepper
Lemon wedges, to serve

SERVES 2

PAPRIKA SALMON

Mix the cumin, paprika and cinnamon together in a bowl. Roll the salmon fillets in the mixture, ensuring they are well coated all over.

Melt the coconut oil in a heavy-based frying pan over a medium heat. Place the salmon in skin-side down and fry for a minute or so until you can see that it's cooked on that side, before turning over and frying the other side until cooked to your liking (bearing in mind it will continue to cook off the heat).

Remove from the heat and leave to stand for 4 minutes before serving, allowing the salmon to continue cooking. Serve with my Ultimate Salad (page 53).

1 tbsp ground cumin
1 tbsp paprika (mild or hot to your taste)
½ tbsp Lucy Bee cinnamon powder
2 salmon fillets
30g/1 oz Lucy Bee coconut oil

SERVES 2

MACADAMIA CRUSTED FISH

Preheat the oven to 180°C/350°F/gas mark 4.

Blitz the macadamia nuts to crumbs in a small food processor, then mix with the breadcrumbs and desiccated coconut. Transfer this to a dish.

Beat the egg and place in a second dish. In a third dish, mix the flour with the chilli flakes, salt and pepper.

Take one piece of fish and dip it first into the flour mixture then the beaten egg, and lastly coat it generously in the nut mixture. Repeat this process with the other piece of fish.

Melt the coconut oil in a heavy-based ovenproof frying pan over a medium heat. When hot, add the fish, turning each piece over after about 3 minutes. Cook the other side for 3 minutes, then transfer to the oven for 10–15 minutes, or until the fish is just cooked through. Serve with my chips and mushy peas (page 99).

125g/1 cup macadamia nuts
40g/¾ cup gluten-free breadcrumbs
25g/⅓ cup desiccated coconut
1 egg
75g/⅔ cup rice flour or gluten-free plain (all-purpose) flour
Pinch of dried chilli flakes
Pinch each of Lucy Bee Himalayan salt and ground black pepper
400g/14 oz fillet of white fish, skinned and cut in half
1–2 tbsp Lucy Bee coconut oil

SERVES 2

CHICKEN BURGER WITH SWEET POTATO WEDGES

This idea came from a lunch I had in London a little while ago and as so often happens, I wanted to put my mark on it. I love all the different flavours, colours and textures. This is a must-have when catching up with friends. Just remember to have your favourite tipple at the ready.

Preheat the oven to 180°C/350°F/gas mark 4. Add the coconut oil for the sweet potato wedges to a roasting tray and place in the oven to heat. Once hot, add the sweet potato wedges and some chilli flakes, if using, and stir through to coat. Bake for 45–50 minutes, turning and checking occasionally, until cooked through and beginning to caramelize at the edges.

Add all the marinade ingredients to a bowl with salt and pepper to taste, stir, then add the chicken breasts. Use your fingers to massage the marinade into the chicken and leave for a few minutes or up to an hour, to allow the flavours to infuse (you can also do this in a sealed food bag if you like).

When ready to cook, place the chicken breasts on a baking tray and cover the tray with foil. Bake in the oven for 20 minutes, then remove the foil and continue to cook for a further 10 minutes or until cooked through.

Serve the burgers whole in the buns, if using, with the avocado and pea dip, coleslaw and lettuce, or try them sliced in a cup of lettuce.

2 boneless, skinless chicken breasts
Lucy Bee Himalayan salt and ground
  black pepper

FOR THE MARINADE
½ tsp sweet smoked paprika
½ tsp cayenne pepper
1 tbsp sesame seeds
1 tbsp Greek yoghurt
Squeeze of lime juice

FOR THE SWEET POTATO WEDGES
1 tbsp Lucy Bee coconut oil
2 large sweet potatoes, cut into
  chunky wedges
Chilli flakes, to season (optional)

TO SERVE
2 gluten-free burger buns or rolls
  (optional)
Avocado and Pea Dip (see page 180)
Fennel and Red Cabbage Coleslaw
  (see page 182)
Lettuce

SERVES 2

CAULIFLOWER RICE WITH PUMPKIN SEEDS

Essentially a side dish but I often have this as a lunch on its own. Since turmeric is so good for us, we're always trying to find tasty ways to add it to meals and this is just perfect, giving this otherwise simple dish a real punch.

Blitz the cauliflower in a food processor until it resembles rice (or finely chop it using a knife).

Melt the coconut oil in a deep frying pan over a medium heat. Add the cauliflower, pumpkin seeds and turmeric and fry, stirring constantly, for 5–10 minutes or until cooked. Season and serve.

400g/14 oz cauliflower, roughly chopped
1 tbsp Lucy Bee coconut oil
60g/scant ½ cup pumpkin seeds
1 tbsp Lucy Bee turmeric powder
Lucy Bee Himalayan salt and ground black pepper

SERVES 1–2

TIP
Add chilli flakes to spice things up, if you like.

PAK CHOI WITH GOJI BERRIES

I've taken this idea from one of my family's most visited Chinese restaurants. The goji berries give it a deliciously sweet kick when paired with the pak choi, or bok choy – either way, it's also known as Chinese cabbage.

Melt the coconut oil in a deep pan or wok over a medium heat. Add the ginger and sauté for 1 minute. Stir in the sesame oil, tamari and vinegar, then add the goji berries and reduce the heat to low.

Simmer for 5 minutes or until the goji berries have softened, then add the honey or maple syrup and stir again. Finally add the water and pak choi (bok choy), cover and simmer for a further 10 minutes. Stir again and serve hot.

1 tbsp Lucy Bee coconut oil
2.5cm/1 in piece of fresh ginger, peeled and finely chopped
1 tbsp sesame oil
2 tbsp tamari sauce
1½ tbsp red wine vinegar
40g/1½ oz goji berries
1 tbsp honey or maple syrup
90ml/¼ cup plus 2 tbsp water
3 pak choi (bok choy), stems separated

SERVES 2

TIP
Try adding a sprinkling of sesame seeds or crushed cashews to serve.

COURGETTE OR MARROW FRIES WITH SESAME SEEDS

Preheat the oven to 180°C/350°F/gas mark 4. Grease a large baking tray with coconut oil.

Thoroughly wash the marrow or courgettes (zucchini) and cut into chunky chip shapes.

Beat the egg in a bowl. In a separate bowl, mix the almond flour, sesame seeds and some seasoning together.

Dip each courgette or marrow chip into the egg, then roll in the flour mixture, transferring them to the greased baking tray in a single layer. Drizzle over the melted coconut oil and bake for 40 minutes, until crisp and golden.

1 tbsp Lucy Bee coconut oil, melted, plus extra for greasing
½ large marrow (vegetable marrow) or 4 small courgettes (zucchini)
1 medium egg
40g/1½ oz almond flour
40g/generous ½ cup sesame seeds
Lucy Bee Himalayan salt and ground black pepper

SERVES 2–4

TIP
Plain (all-purpose) flour is fine instead of almond flour, if there's no need to be gluten-free.

TWICE-BAKED CARROT FRIES

Preheat the oven to 180°C/350°F/gas mark 4.

Put the carrots into a large baking tray with the melted coconut oil and toss in the oil to coat the carrots all over. Spread out in an even layer and bake in the oven for 10 minutes to soften.

Meanwhile, in a mixing bowl, stir together the flour, sesame seeds and some seasoning.

Take the tray out of the oven and sprinkle the flour mixture over the carrots, turning them to make sure they are all coated. Leave to stand for 10 minutes, allowing the flour to set onto the carrots and cool slightly, and increase the oven temperature to 200°C/400°F/gas mark 6. Put the carrots back in the oven and bake for a further 25–30 minutes, until crisp.

4 large carrots, peeled and cut into chunky chips
2 tbsp Lucy Bee coconut oil, melted
1 tbsp gram flour or gluten-free plain (all-purpose) flour
1 tbsp sesame seeds
Lucy Bee Himalayan salt and ground black pepper

SERVES 2

CRUNCHY BROCCOLI AND STEAK SALAD WITH BLUE CHEESE SAUCE

Don't they say that the way to a man's heart is through his stomach? Well this one should definitely hit the spot!

Cook the broccoli in a shallow pan of boiling water for 2 minutes, to soften slightly, then drain.

Melt the coconut oil in a frying pan or griddle pan, add the garlic and sauté for 1 minute before adding the asparagus and drained broccoli. Fry for 5 minutes then turn over and fry for 5 minutes on the other side, until the broccoli florets are crisp. Remove to 2 serving plates and keep warm.

Meanwhile, to make the blue cheese sauce, put the coconut oil, flour and milk in a small saucepan over a low heat. Stir continuously until the sauce thickens then stir in the cheese. Pour into a jug or gravy boat and keep warm.

While the broccoli pan is still hot, place the steaks in the centre of the pan, season and cook on both sides for 2 minutes (for medium rare).

To serve, slice the steaks into strips using a sharp knife, place on top of the vegetables and pour the sauce over.

200g/7 oz purple sprouting broccoli, ends trimmed
1 tsp Lucy Bee coconut oil
2 garlic cloves, chopped
100g/3½ oz asparagus, woody ends removed
2 sirloin steaks
Lucy Bee Himalayan salt and ground black pepper

FOR THE SAUCE

30g/1 oz Lucy Bee coconut oil
1 tbsp gluten-free plain (all-purpose) flour
150ml/½ cup plus 2 tbsp milk
70g/2½ oz blue cheese, diced

SERVES 2

TIP
We've opted for sirloin here as it is full of flavour but feel free to use your favourite cut.

ROASTED VEGETABLES WITH TURMERIC

Turmeric is a great anti-inflammatory and is best absorbed by the body when used with a fat such as coconut oil, and also black pepper. So this is a win-win.

Preheat the oven to 200°C/400°F/gas mark 7.

Peel the vegetables. Cut sweet potatoes, carrots, parsnips, pumpkins, beetroot and swede into about 5cm/2 in cubes.

Put the melted coconut oil in a large mixing bowl and add the turmeric, salt and pepper. Add the vegetables and mix everything together thoroughly. Spread out on a large baking tray and roast in the oven for about 50 minutes or until the vegetables are soft (especially the sweet potatoes), turning them halfway through.

1.5kg (3¼ lb) vegetables, such as sweet potatoes, carrots, parsnips, pumpkin, beetroot, swede, cauliflower and broccoli florets
2 tbsp Lucy Bee coconut oil, melted
1 tsp Lucy Bee turmeric powder
¼ tsp each of Lucy Bee Himalayan salt and ground black pepper

SERVES 4

> **TIP**
> If you find the vegetables are starting to burn, turn the oven temperature down and cook for a little longer; you want the vegetables tasting sweet.

MATCHA AND BANANA LOAF CAKE

With such incredible health benefits, we were keen to look at different ways to incorporate matcha into our diets and this cake ticks all the boxes. With its hint of green colour, you just know that this truly is 'having your cake and eating it'.

Preheat the oven to 160°C/320°F/gas mark 3. Line a 450g/1lb loaf tin with baking parchment.

Using an electric whisk, mix together the eggs and banana, then add the yoghurt, vanilla and melted coconut oil and whisk until combined.

Mix all the dry ingredients together well in another bowl, then add the wet ingredients and stir until thoroughly combined. Pour the mixture into the prepared tin and smooth the surface with a spatula. Bake in the oven for 45 minutes until a skewer inserted into the middle comes out clean, then leave to cool in the tin.

3 eggs
2 ripe bananas, puréed
100g/3½ oz plain yoghurt
1 tsp vanilla extract
140g/5 oz Lucy Bee coconut oil, melted
200g/1½ cups gluten-free plain (all-purpose) flour
100g/3½ oz ground pistachios
150g/¾ cup coconut sugar
2 tbsp matcha powder
1 tsp bicarbonate of soda
1 tsp gluten-free baking powder
1 tsp Lucy Bee cinnamon powder

SERVES 6–8

SATURDAY NIGHT FAKEAWAYS

Sometimes a little indulgence is just what you need at the weekend, or even during the week! This chapter's title says it all, but this is where you'll find our healthier take on our favourite dishes from takeaway places. We have travelled around the world (in the Lucy Bee kitchen) to bring you Chicken Katsu Curry, classic gluten-free Pizza, Fish, Chips and Mushy Peas and Sweet and Sour Chicken. Guilt-free takeaways? I'll be ordering – I mean cooking – one of those!

SHAKSHUKA

Line a large baking sheet with kitchen paper, place the aubergine slices on top and sprinkle salt lightly and evenly all over the cut surfaces. Set aside for 30 minutes then, using kitchen paper, wipe away the salt, and the water which has been released.

Place a heavy-based frying pan (that has a lid) over a medium heat, add the coconut oil and, when hot add the onion and cook until translucent, then add the garlic and fry for a further minute or so.

Cut the aubergine slices into quarters and add to the pan with the potato. Fry for another couple of minutes, then add the tomatoes, water, tomato purée (paste), oregano, turmeric, cumin, chilli flakes and a pinch of black pepper. Cover and simmer for around 20–25 minutes, until the potatoes are cooked and the aubergines soft. Taste and add salt if needed.

Serve the shakshuka with plain yoghurt and some crusty bread.

2 medium aubergines (eggplants), sliced into rounds 2cm (¾ in) thick
2 tbsp Lucy Bee coconut oil
1 medium onion, diced
3 garlic cloves, finely chopped
1 large potato, peeled and cut into 2cm (¾ in) cubes
2 x 400g tins/4 cups chopped tomatoes
120ml/½ cup water
1 tbsp tomato purée (paste)
1 tsp fresh or dried oregano
1 tsp Lucy Bee turmeric powder
1 tsp ground cumin
Pinch of chilli flakes
Lucy Bee Himalayan salt and ground black pepper

SERVES 6

LAHMACUN (TURKISH PIZZA)

Preheat the oven to 200°C/400°F/gas mark 6. Line 2 large baking sheets with baking parchment.

In a food processor, blend together the (bell) peppers, onion, garlic and parsley. Line a colander or sieve with a clean tea towel, spoon the mixture into the tea towel and squeeze to drain out most of the moisture (don't waste it – add some ice and drink it or save/freeze to use in soups, as a stock).

Put the mince and the remaining ingredients, including the blended peppers, into a large bowl and mix to a paste-like mixture. Traditionally, you would do this using your hands, but you can use a large wooden spoon if you prefer.

Spread a very thin layer of topping onto each socca or pitta base, making sure it's not too thick. Transfer the lahmacuns to the lined baking sheets and bake in the oven for 5–10 minutes or until cooked.

To serve, squeeze over some lemon juice and sprinkle with chopped parsley.

3 red and 2 green peppers (bell peppers), quartered and deseeded
1 large onion, peeled and quartered
1 garlic clove, peeled
50g/1¾ oz flat-leaf parsley, plus an extra handful, chopped, to serve
500g/1lb 1oz lean minced beef
1 x 400g tin/1 cup chopped tomatoes
½ tsp paprika (mild or hot)
Pinch of chilli flakes
Pinch each of Lucy Bee Himalayan salt and ground black pepper
Squeeze of lemon juice, to serve
1 quantity cooked Socca pancakes (see page 80) or 6 gluten-free pitta breads, halved

MAKES 12

LENTILS AND CAULIFLOWER

Cauliflower has made such a comeback from those days when all anyone did was boil it! Lentils are an inexpensive source of protein and are really filling too – perfect for meat-free Mondays. This combination works so well together as part of a satisfying, nutritious meal any day of the week.

Heat the coconut oil in a large frying pan that has a lid and, when hot, add the onions and sauté for about 5 minutes over a medium heat until soft, taking care not to let them brown.

Blitz the garlic, ginger and water together in a small food processor, then add to the onions and stir to mix. Stir in the cauliflower, lentils, cumin and cardamom seeds, chilli, turmeric and stock.

Bring to the boil, then turn down the heat so the mixture is gently bubbling away. Cover and cook for 10 minutes, then remove the lid and continue to cook for a further 10 minutes, adding a little water if the mixture becomes too dry. Serve hot as a side dish.

30g/1 oz Lucy Bee coconut oil
300g/10½ oz onions, chopped
2 garlic cloves, peeled
About 40g/1½ oz fresh ginger, peeled
50ml/scant ¼ cup water
1 medium-sized cauliflower, cut into small florets
100g/½ cup red lentils
1 tsp cumin seeds
Seeds of 3 cardamom pods
Pinch of chilli powder, or more depending on how much heat you want
1 tsp Lucy Bee turmeric powder
700ml/scant 3 cups vegetable stock (see page 176 for homemade)

SERVES 4

(see page 176 for homemade)

TIP
For a nutritious breakfast, serve any leftovers the next morning with a poached egg.

SPICED PRAWNS

Who needs a takeaway when you have this home-cooked curry? Perfect for sharing with friends and catching up on who's been doing what over the week.

Heat the coconut oil in a heavy-based frying pan, add the onions and sauté until soft, then add the garlic, ginger, chillies, all the seeds and the turmeric. Stir everything together and cook for 1 minute, then add the tomatoes and simmer for 10–15 minutes over a low heat, stirring occasionally and allowing the mixture to reduce.

Add the prawns (shrimp), bring to the boil, lower the heat and allow the prawns to cook, about 3–5 minutes, stirring occasionally. Now turn the heat to high and reduce the sauce to a thick consistency. Stir in the garam masala and coriander (cilantro), season to taste and serve with lemon wedges.

2 tbsp Lucy Bee coconut oil
125g/4½ oz onions, finely chopped
2–3 garlic cloves, finely chopped
40g/1½ oz fresh ginger, peeled and grated
2 green chillies, deseeded and roughly chopped
2 tsp each of nigella seeds, mustard seeds, cumin seeds and fenugreek seeds
1 tsp Lucy Bee turmeric powder
1 x 400g tin/200g chopped tomatoes
500g/1lb 1 oz raw prawns (shrimp), peeled and deveined
1 tsp garam masala
Big bunch of fresh coriander (cilantro), chopped
Lucy Bee Himalayan salt and ground black pepper
Lemons wedges, to serve

SERVES 4

TIP
Keep any leftovers in the fridge and add to a salad or omelette for a tasty, quick lunch.

CHICKPEA CURRY WITH POTATOES AND MUSHROOMS

I love the differing textures in this curry, from the firmness of the mushrooms to the smoother bite of the potatoes, which when combined, make this a satisfying meal. An added bonus is that it's packed full of goodness that will keep you feeling fuller for longer.

Heat the coconut oil in a wide frying pan, add the onions, garlic and ginger and sauté for a few minutes until the onions are soft. Stir in the spices, then add the potatoes, mushrooms, chickpeas (garbanzo beans) and stock. Stir everything together, then bring to the boil, cover and reduce to a simmer for 15 minutes.

Remove the lid, increase the heat and continue to simmer for a further 10–15 minutes, until the liquid is reduced to a nice, thick sauce and the potatoes are cooked. Check for seasoning and add salt if needed. Stir in the chopped coriander (cilantro) and serve.

50g/1¾ oz Lucy Bee coconut oil
200g/7 oz onions, roughly chopped
2 garlic cloves, chopped
40g/1½ oz fresh ginger, peeled and grated
2 tbsp curry powder (see page 177 for homemade)
1 tsp ground coriander
½ tsp Lucy Bee cinnamon powder
1 tsp Lucy Bee turmeric powder
340g/12 oz potatoes, peeled and chopped into cubes
250g/8¾ oz chestnut mushrooms, washed and cut into quarters
1 x 400g tin/1¾ cups chickpeas (garbanzo beans), drained and rinsed
500ml/2 cups plus 1 tbsp vegetable stock (see page 176 for homemade)
Handful of coriander (cilantro), roughly chopped
Lucy Bee Himalayan salt

SERVES 4–6

SOCCA WITH AVOCADO, ASPARAGUS AND POACHED EGG

A naturally gluten-free pancake-cum-flatbread, which originates from Italy, socca is a great substitute to have for breakfast, instead of toast. This traditional street food also has a place in French kitchens and is often served as a side with olives, dips and cheese.

Preheat the oven to 170°C/325°F/gas mark 3. Line 2 baking sheets with baking parchment.

For the socca, place the chickpea (gram) flour, turmeric, salt and pepper in a large bowl and mix well. Add the water and melted coconut oil and whisk by hand until all the ingredients are well combined. Using an electric hand-held whisk, whisk the egg whites to soft peaks then gently fold the whites into the chickpea flour batter. Set aside for 10 minutes.

Meanwhile, mash the avocados using a fork, sprinkle with lemon juice and black pepper and set aside.

Melt a little coconut oil in a large non-stick frying pan over a high heat, then reduce the heat to medium. Using a ladle, pour in 2 generous spoonsful of the chickpea batter to make a pancake and cook for 2–3 minutes until air bubbles appear on the top and the bottom has set. Turn the pancake over carefully and cook for a further 2 minutes, then transfer to one of the lined baking sheets. Repeat until you have used all the batter, then transfer the baking sheets to the oven for 5–6 minutes.

While the pancakes are baking, steam or simmer the asparagus spears in water for 4–5 minutes and poach the eggs in hot water for 2–4 minutes so that the white is cooked and the yolk is runny, allowing one egg per person.

Remove the socca from the oven and spread with the mashed avocado. Place a few asparagus spears on top of the avocado then carefully place a poached egg on top of the asparagus spears. Grind a little black pepper over the egg and serve.

FOR THE SOCCA PANCAKES

1½ tbsp Lucy Bee coconut oil, melted, plus extra for cooking
230g/1¾ cups chickpea (gram) flour
1 tsp Lucy Bee turmeric powder
½ tsp each of Lucy Bee Himalayan salt and ground black pepper
450ml/scant 2 cups water
2 egg whites

FOR THE TOPPING

3 avocados
Lemon juice
Ground black pepper
200g/7 oz asparagus
4–6 eggs

SERVES 4

GF WF LF DF V VEG

CHAPATI

Finally, I can enjoy these traditional Indian breads with my curries! If you're coeliac or just want to avoid gluten, I'm sure you'll enjoy these as much as I do. 'Chapat' means 'to slap' which aptly describes how to make these – slap the dough down to flatten as you then turn and repeat.

Put the flour and mashed potato into a large mixing bowl and rub together between your fingertips until it forms a breadcrumb-like mixture and there are no big lumps.

Add the 2 tsp melted coconut oil and 50ml/scant ¼ cup of the warm water to the flour and potato mixture and mix in using your hands. When it starts to form a ball of dough, add the rest of the water and knead until all the crumbs are mixed in. Knead the dough for a further 3 minutes then set aside.

Wipe the work surface clean with a wet cloth and place a small sheet of cling film on it; the moisture will help the cling film to stick to the surface and make it easier to lift your chapatis into the pan.

Divide the dough into 7 balls and place one on top of the cling film. Place another small piece of cling film over the top and roll out the dough to a round about 10cm/4 in diameter.

Heat 1 tsp of the coconut oil in a frying pan. Remove the top piece of cling film and, using the bottom piece to lift the chapati, invert it into the frying pan. Cook until bubbles start to form then flip it over and cook the other side until there are a few brown spots. Repeat with the remaining dough, adding the remaining coconut oil as needed.

240g/1¾ cups gluten-free plain (all-purpose) flour
70g/2½ oz mashed potato
2 tsp Lucy Bee coconut oil, melted, plus 3 tsp for frying
100ml/scant ½ cup warm water

MAKES 7

TIP
These freeze well so you can make a batch ahead of time and defrost as needed.

GF WF LF DF V VEG

CHICKEN KATSU CURRY

Originally a Japanese meal, chicken katsu curries have become very popular everywhere – even my local town has its own restaurant serving katsu curry now.
If you haven't come across this dish before I'm sure you'll soon be a real fan and, as you've probably guessed, we've added our own gluten-free twist on it.

For the chicken, mix 1tsp of curry powder and chickpea (gram) flour together in a bowl and add the salt and pepper. Put the beaten egg into a separate bowl and the breadcrumbs into a third bowl.

Dust each chicken breast first in the seasoned flour, then the egg, followed by the breadcrumbs to coat. Set aside while you make the sauce.

Melt the coconut oil in a heavy-based saucepan over a low heat, add the onions, ginger and carrots and cook for a few minutes until the onions begin to soften, stirring to make sure they don't burn. Add the garlic and sauté for 1 minute, adding a little more coconut oil if necessary.

Stir in 1 tbsp curry powder and chickpea flour and mix everything together thoroughly. Add the stock gradually, stirring continuously. Add the honey, bay leaf and tamari, bring to a gentle simmer, cover and cook over a low heat for 20 minutes, or until the vegetables are soft (which may take a little longer). Use a hand-held blender or food processor to blend into a smooth sauce.

While the sauce is simmering, cook the rice according to the packet instructions and preheat the oven to 180°C/350°F/gas mark 4.

To cook the chicken, heat the coconut oil in an ovenproof frying pan. When hot, place the chicken breasts in the pan and cook for about 3 minutes on each side, then transfer the pan to the oven for about 10 minutes until cooked through (I use a Thermapen to check; it should read 75°C/165°F in the centre).

Remove the chicken from the pan, cut the breasts into slices, place the slices on a plate with the rice and pour over the sauce. Sprinkle over the chopped coriander (cilantro) to serve.

FOR THE CHICKEN

1 tsp plus 1 tbsp curry powder (see page 177 for homemade)
50g/⅓ cup chickpea (gram) flour
Pinch each of Lucy Bee Himalayan salt and ground black pepper
1 egg, beaten
60g/1 cup gluten-free breadcrumbs
2 boneless, skinless chicken breasts
30g/1oz Lucy Bee coconut oil

FOR THE SAUCE

30g/1oz Lucy Bee coconut oil
150g/5¼ oz onions, chopped
50g/1¾ oz fresh ginger, peeled and grated or blitzed
2 medium carrots, diced
3 garlic cloves, crushed
1 tbsp chickpea (gram) flour
375ml/generous 1½ cups chicken stock (see page 177 for homemade)
2 tsp honey
1 bay leaf
1 tbsp tamari sauce

TO SERVE

150g/generous 1 cup brown rice
Chopped coriander (cilantro)

SERVES 2

SMOKY TOFU OR CHICKEN FAJITAS

Truly a 'recipe for real life' this was originally the meal that Mexican cowboys cooked up having been given the throwaway cuts of meat as part of their wages. Today we enjoy fajitas with family and friends, gathered around the table and revel in the party atmosphere while everyone has their own style for building up their fajita.

To make the salsa, put the red onion and lime juice in a bowl and leave to marinate for at least 15 minutes, or as long as overnight (the longer you do the sweeter and softer the onion will be). Stir in the tomatoes.

Melt the coconut oil in a frying pan over a medium heat, add the tofu (beancurd) or chicken with the paprika and chilli powder and fry for 6–8 minutes, stirring continuously. Add the (bell) pepper, onion and garlic and fry for another 2–3 minutes before adding the kidney beans. Cook for a further 2 minutes or until the chicken (if using) is cooked through.

For the guacamole, mash together the avocado, chilli flakes, if using, and lemon juice.

To assemble the fajitas, layer them up as you prefer – I like to add lettuce then salsa to the centre of the wrap, followed by guacamole, then tofu or chicken and Greek yoghurt on top.

1 tbsp Lucy Bee coconut oil
200g/7 oz tofu (beancurd) or
    2 boneless, skinless chicken
    breasts, sliced
1 tsp sweet smoked paprika
1 tsp chilli powder
1 red pepper (bell pepper), deseeded
    and sliced
1 onion, diced
2 garlic cloves, chopped
1 x 400g tin/1⅔ cups kidney beans,
    drained

FOR THE SALSA
1 small red onion, chopped
Juice of 1 lime
6–8 cherry tomatoes, quartered

FOR THE GUACAMOLE
1 avocado
1 tsp chilli flakes (optional)
Juice of 1 lemon wedge

TO SERVE
4 gluten-free wraps
Lettuce leaves
2 tbsp Greek yoghurt

SERVES 2

FISH TACOS WITH COCONUT LIME CREAM

On paper this might look a bit more challenging but it's actually surprisingly simple to make and delicious to eat. A word of warning with this one though, it can get a bit messy to eat so not an ideal first-date dinner!

Preheat the oven to 180°C/350°F/gas mark 4.

Mix the chopped garlic, lime juice, ¼ tsp cumin and chilli flakes in a dish, add the fish and leave to marinate for 15–20 minutes.

Meanwhile, for the black bean sauce, melt the coconut oil in a deep frying pan or saucepan, add the onions and sauté for 5 minutes or until translucent, then add the crushed garlic and sauté for a further minute. Add the black (turtle) beans, coconut butter if using, water, chopped tomatoes, ½ tsp cumin and paprika and bring to the boil. Once the sauce begins to bubble, reduce the heat and simmer for 20 minutes.

While the black bean sauce is simmering, put the lime juice, coconut cream, water and a pinch of salt in a bowl and mix together well.

Transfer the fish and marinade to a baking tray, add salt and pepper to taste and bake for 20 minutes or until cooked through. Once cooked, shred the fish into a dish and place all the serving ingredients in separate dishes, for everyone to help themselves and build their own wrap.

500g/1lb 1oz haddock fillet
4 garlic cloves, 2 chopped and
   2 crushed
Juice of 1 lime
¾ tsp ground cumin
¼ tsp dried chilli flakes
Lucy Bee Himalayan salt and ground
   black pepper
1 tbsp Lucy Bee coconut oil
100g/3½ oz onions, chopped
1 x 400g tin/1⅔ cup black (turtle)
   beans, drained and rinsed
30g/1oz coconut butter (optional)
150ml/½ cup plus 2 tbsp water
½ x 400g tin/1 cup chopped tomatoes
1 tsp smoked paprika

FOR THE COCONUT LIME CREAM
Juice of ½–1 lime
160ml tin/⅔ cup coconut cream
120ml/½ cup water

TO SERVE
Gluten-free wraps or tortillas
Little gem lettuce
Chopped avocado
Chopped fresh coriander (cilantro)
Shredded red cabbage

SERVES 4

TIP
Black bean sauce freezes well.

COURGETTI CARBONARA

This is my healthier take on this popular Italian dish and it just had to be courgetti, the modern foodie's go-to spaghetti.

Add the pancetta to a deep frying pan and lightly sauté over a medium heat until cooked, then add the garlic and cook until golden. Remove the pan from the heat and set aside.

Put the yoghurt, eggs, 20g/¾ oz of the Parmesan and the parsley in a bowl and, using a hand-held whisk, mix together.

Place the pan with pancetta back over a low heat, add the courgettes, mix and cook for 1 minute before stirring in the egg mixture. Combine well and serve with the remaining grated Parmesan and salt and pepper to taste.

80g/2¾ oz pancetta
1–2 garlic cloves, finely chopped
40g/1½ oz Greek yoghurt
2 eggs
30g/1oz Parmesan, grated
1 tsp finely chopped parsley
2–3 courgettes (zucchini), either spiralized or cut lengthways into very fine shreds
Lucy Bee Himalayan salt and ground black pepper

SERVES 2

TIP
Although we use courgetti here for a healthy, gluten-free twist, brown rice pasta is also great in its place for a more filling dish!

PIZZA MESS – MADE FOR SHARING!

Good hangover food or perfect for when you are in the mood for a mouth-watering brunch. Feel free to swap the toppings for any of your particular favourites.

Preheat the oven to 180°C/350°F/gas mark 4.

Place the grated sweet potato in the middle of a sheet of kitchen paper, wrap and press firmly to squeeze out excess water. Add the sweet potato to a bowl with the onion, rosemary and some salt and pepper, and mix well.

Melt the coconut oil in a medium roasting tray in the oven and, when hot, add the sweet potato mixture, spread out in an even layer and bake in the oven for 15 minutes.

Meanwhile, cook the peas in boiling water until tender, then drain and set aside.

Remove the sweet potato from the oven and top with, in order: the peas, basil, tomatoes, mozzarella, chilli flakes, if using, and some seasoning. Return to the oven for a further 6–8 minutes until the mozzarella has melted and the sweet potato is crunchy. Remove from the oven and serve from the tray, with a drizzle of pesto on top.

600g/1lb 5 oz sweet potatoes, peeled and grated
1 red onion, finely chopped
1 tsp dried rosemary
1 tbsp Lucy Bee coconut oil
50g/1¾ oz frozen peas
Handful of fresh basil
6 cherry tomatoes, quartered
60g/2 oz mozzarella, sliced
Pinch of chilli flakes, to taste (optional)
Lucy Bee Himalayan salt and ground black pepper
Drizzle of green pesto (for homemade see page 105), to serve

SERVES 4

PIZZA – THE CLASSIC

As I mentioned in the introduction, my friends always preferred my gluten-free pizza to their store-bought ones so I'm really happy to be able to share this with you all. As with a lot of my recipes, feel free to switch the toppings to your own favourites.

Preheat the oven to 220°C/425°F/gas mark 7. Lightly oil a non-stick baking tray with coconut oil.

Put the tomatoes, tomato purée (paste), mixed herbs and some salt and pepper in a frying pan and bring to the boil, then turn the heat down to low, stir and continue to cook, stirring occasionally, until the mixture has thickened to a paste, about 15 minutes.

Meanwhile, for the dough, put the melted coconut oil, flour, yeast, water, ½ tsp salt and a pinch of pepper into a food processor and blitz until combined into a dough.

Knead the dough on a floured surface for about 3 minutes, then roll it out onto a non-stick baking tray, using your fingers to create a shape for the pizza (I never have the same shape twice!).

Spread the tomato mixture over the base, place the mozzarella slices on top along with the topping or toppings of your choice and cook in the oven for 12–15 minutes. Serve immediately.

50g/1¾ oz Lucy Bee coconut oil, melted, plus extra for greasing
1 x 400g tin/2 cups chopped tomatoes
1 tbsp tomato purée (paste)
1 tsp mixed herbs
200g/1½ cups gluten-free plain (all-purpose) flour, plus extra for dusting
10g/⅓ oz easy-bake dried yeast
120ml/½ cup cold water
1 mozzarella ball (125g/4½ oz), sliced
Lucy Bee Himalayan salt and ground black pepper

TOPPING OPTIONS

Anchovy fillets in oil
Olives
Sliced pepperoni
Sliced chorizo
Jalapeños

SERVES 2

SWEET AND SOUR CHICKEN

Dice the chicken, then in a bowl, mix the diced chicken with the egg white, sesame oil, cornflour (cornstarch), salt and pepper. Cover and chill in the fridge for about 20 minutes. Blitz or finely chop half of the pineapple chunks, leaving the remaining half intact, and set aside.

Heat 1 tbsp of the coconut oil in a deep non-stick frying pan over a medium heat and, when hot, add the (bell) pepper and stir-fry for 5 minutes. Remove from the pan and place in a dish.

Add the remaining coconut oil to the frying pan and, when hot, add the ginger, spring onions (scallions), garlic, chilli, star anise and chicken and stir-fry for 5 minutes, before adding the tamarind, rice wine vinegar and 2 tbsp water, with the cooked red pepper, pineapple chunks and blitzed or chopped pineapple. Gently simmer for 10 minutes, until the sauce becomes nice and thick. Turn up the heat and cook until the chicken is cooked through, stirring occasionally. Serve with Prawn Toast (see below), if you like.

2 boneless, skinless chicken breasts
1 egg white
½ tsp sesame oil
2 tsp cornflour (cornstarch)
Pinch each of Lucy Bee Himalayan salt and ground black pepper
400g/14 oz fresh pineapple, chopped
2 tbsp Lucy Bee coconut oil
1 red pepper (bell pepper), deseeded and diced
1 tbsp freshly grated ginger
4 spring onions (scallions), sliced
1 garlic clove, finely chopped
1 red chilli, deseeded and finely chopped
3 star anise
1 tbsp tamarind
50ml/scant ¼ cup rice wine vinegar

SERVES 2

PRAWN TOAST

This is another family favourite, so it was only right to come up with our own gluten-free version!

Blitz the prawns (shrimp), ginger, spring onion (scallion), cornflour (cornstarch), tamari, egg, salt and pepper together in a blender.

Cut the bread slices into the required finger-food size. Spread the prawn mixture on one side then sprinkle sesame seeds over the top. Chill in the fridge for 30 minutes.

Heat enough coconut oil in a deep frying pan for shallow-frying and, when hot, add the prawn toasts and fry on both sides until golden.

150g/5¼ oz peeled prawns (shrimp)
3cm/1¼ in piece of fresh ginger, peeled and roughly chopped
1 spring onion (scallion) or mild onion, roughly chopped
1 tbsp cornflour (cornstarch)
½ tbsp tamari sauce
½ small beaten egg
Pinch each of Lucy Bee Himalayan salt and ground black pepper
6 thin slices of gluten-free bread, crusts removed
Sesame seeds, to sprinkle
Lucy Bee coconut oil, for shallow-frying

SERVES 4

GINGER PORK BALLS IN BROTH WITH RICE NOODLES

Before you pick up the phone to order a takeaway, try this instead – I'm sure you won't be disappointed. It works well as a broth without meat balls too, for those who are vegetarian.

Peel the ginger and grate the flesh (reserve for the pork balls) then add the ginger skin, star anise and lemongrass stalk, if using, to the hot stock. Leave to stand for 30 minutes or longer so it absorbs all the flavours of the spices.

Mix the pork mince, grated ginger and breadcrumbs together with some salt and pepper then, using your hands, form the mixture into about 40 balls. Heat the coconut oil in a frying pan, add the pork balls and cook for 8–10 minutes, turning so they brown evenly all over. Remove from the heat.

Meanwhile, strain the stock to remove the spices, then pour it back into the saucepan and bring to the boil. In a separate pan, cook the noodles according to the instructions on the packet, then drain. Add the tamari, rice wine vinegar, sesame oil and all the vegetables to the boiling stock and, when it starts to gently bubble again, add the pork balls and cook for 5 minutes. Remove from the heat and stir in the coriander (cilantro).

If you have space in the pan, add the drained noodles and stir, otherwise place the noodles in serving bowls and ladle over the pork balls, vegetables and stock. Serve with chopped spring onions (scallions), chilli and sesame oil sprinkled over the top.

80–100g/2¾–3½ oz fresh ginger
6 star anise
1 lemongrass stalk (optional)
2 litres/8½ cups weak hot chicken or vegetable stock (see pages 177 and 176 for homemade)
500g/1lb 1 oz pork mince
50g/1 cup gluten-free breadcrumbs
10g/⅓ oz Lucy Bee coconut oil
200g/7 oz rice noodles
1 tbsp tamari sauce
1 tbsp rice wine vinegar
1 tbsp sesame oil
1 red pepper (bell pepper), about 140g/ 5 oz, deseeded and thinly sliced
200g/7 oz carrots, peeled and cut into matchsticks
200g/7 oz fennel, thinly sliced
225g/8 oz pak choi (bok choy) or cabbage, sliced
Handful of coriander (cilantro), chopped
Lucy Bee Himalayan salt and ground black pepper

TO SERVE
Spring onions (scallions), chopped
Red chilli, chopped
Sesame oil

SERVES 4

FISH, CHIPS AND MUSHY PEAS

A classic British staple, fish and chips were one of the few foods that weren't rationed during World War Two, apparently. Some say they taste better eaten out of paper but here I've opted for a plate instead!

Preheat the oven to 200°C/400°F/gas mark 6 and place a large baking tray in the oven.

Put the beaten egg in a shallow dish and put the rice flour, with a pinch each of salt and pepper, in a second shallow dish. Dip each piece of fish first into the egg, coating it well, then in the seasoned flour, shaking off any excess flour. Set aside in the fridge.

Peel the potatoes and cut them into chips. Bring a pan of water to the boil, add the chips, bring it back to the boil and cook for 3 minutes. Drain then add the coconut oil, which will melt quickly. Gently toss the chips in the oil so they are all coated. Spread the chips out evenly over the hot baking tray and cook in the oven for 20–30 minutes until crisp and golden, checking and turning them every 5–10 minutes.

When the chips have been in the oven for 10 minutes, melt the coconut oil for the peas in a saucepan, add the peas, cover and cook over a medium heat for about 4 minutes or until cooked, stirring occasionally. Add the yoghurt, a squeeze of lemon juice and some salt and pepper. Mash using a potato masher, adding more seasoning and lemon juice if required. Keep warm while you cook the fish.

Heat the coconut oil in a deep, heavy-based frying pan over a medium heat and, when hot, add the fish and cook for about 3 minutes, then turn and cook for a further 3–5 minutes, until just cooked through (check with a sharp knife inserted into the middle, and bearing in mind it will continue to cook off the heat).

Remove from the heat and let the fish sit in the frying pan for 3 minutes before serving with the chips, mushy peas and lemon wedges.

FOR THE FISH
1 medium egg, beaten
4 tbsp rice flour
400g/14 oz cod loin, cut into
    2 pieces
40g/1½ oz Lucy Bee coconut oil
Lucy Bee Himalayan salt and ground
    black pepper
Lemon wedges, to serve

FOR THE CHIPS
500g/1lb 1 oz potatoes, ideally
    Maris Piper, King Edward or
    Roosters (my favourite)
1 tbsp Lucy Bee coconut oil

FOR THE MUSHY PEAS
1 tsp Lucy Bee coconut oil
200g/generous 1½ cups frozen peas
30g/1 oz Greek yoghurt or lactose-
    free yoghurt
Lemon juice, to taste

SERVES 2

CLASSIC BURGERS

Jazz up this easy-to-make burger simply by adding different toppings to it such as jalapeños, cheeses, avocado, gherkins, bacon, rocket, iceberg lettuce, chives or pesto. A Thermapen or meat thermometer is great for making sure your meat is cooked to your liking, so this is one gadget I'd really recommend investing in.

Place the beef mince and mustard or horseradish and herbs, if using, in a mixing bowl. Add plenty of ground black pepper and, using your hands, combine all the ingredients and shape into 4 equal-sized burgers.

Place a heavy-based frying pan or griddle pan over a medium-high heat, add the coconut oil to the pan and, when hot, sprinkle Himalayan salt over your burger and place salt-side down in the pan. Leave to cook for 5 minutes then sprinkle over a little salt before turning and cooking for a further 5 minutes, depending on how well cooked you like your burger (see tip below). You can also cook the burgers on a preheated outdoor barbecue.

If serving with cheese, add a slice to the top of each burger and allow to cook for a few minutes, until the cheese melts a little. Toast the buns, if you wish, before assembling the burgers with the toppings of your choice.

500g/1lb 1oz Aberdeen Angus beef mince
1 tbsp Dijon mustard or horseradish (optional)
30g/1 oz chopped coriander (cilantro) or parsley (optional)
1–2 tsp Lucy Bee coconut oil
Lucy Bee Himalayan salt and ground black pepper

SERVING OPTIONS

4 gluten-free burger buns or rolls
4 slices of cheese
Mayonnaise (see page 181)
Homemade Tomato Ketchup (see page 181)
Lettuce
Thin slices of red onion
Sliced beef tomato
Jalapeños

SERVES 4

TIP
Burgers in our house are a real summer thing to enjoy with friends, but cooking them to everyone's liking is tricky, which is where the Thermapen, or meat thermometer, comes in very handy. For well-done meat the internal temperature should be 70°C/158°F and for medium-rare about 60°C/42°F.

GF WF LF DF V VEG

SHARING IS CARING

These meals are perfect for when you've got a little bit more time on your hands and are looking for something to satisfy everyone around the table. We've got a spin on some classics, as well as some suggestions that will have you thinking a bit more outside the box. So, whether you're sitting down with a group of friends or winding down with family. I'm sure they will all love the Steak and Garlic in Red Wine, Chicken Pie or Gardener's Pie as much as we do!

BRUSSELS SPROUT, CHESTNUT AND APRICOT STIR FRY

Most people I've mentioned this recipe to can't quite get their head around it, until they've tried it. Fear not, it's delicious and is a must-try. Sprouts have become very popular again recently and with good reason too since they pack a mighty nutritional punch.

Cook the noodles in boiling water according to the packet instructions, then drain and rinse.

Heat the coconut oil in a wok or high-sided frying pan over a medium heat. When hot, add the sprouts, onion and garlic and cook for 5–6 minutes, or until soft, stirring occasionally. Add the apricots, pomegranate seeds, chestnuts, sesame oil and tamari and continue stirring and cooking for 3 minutes, to combine the flavours.

Add the drained (or fresh) noodles to the wok or pan, give it a final mix and serve.

150g/5¼ oz dried rice noodles
1 tbsp Lucy Bee coconut oil
150g/5¼ oz Brussels sprouts, outer leaves removed, quartered
1 red onion, diced
2 garlic cloves, finely chopped
50g/1¾ oz soft dried apricots, quartered
50g/1¾ oz pomegranate seeds
30g/1 oz pre-cooked chestnuts, quartered
1 tbsp sesame oil
1 tbsp tamari sauce

SERVES 2

TIP
If you're a fish lover, this works well with prawns (shrimp).

SPICY CHICKEN

This recipe is in response to the question: 'how many different ways can you cook chicken?'! It's quick and simple and oh so tasty too. If you have any of the pesto left over, try using it on a fillet of salmon or storing it in the fridge to stir into pasta.

Preheat the oven to 180°C/350°F/gas mark 4.

Put all the pesto ingredients except the pine nuts and lemon zest into a small food processor or blender and blitz together, then stir in the pine nuts and lemon zest.

Slice each chicken breast across horizontally, cutting almost but not completely through, to make a pocket. Fill each pocket with a quarter of the pesto mixture and place the stuffed breasts in an ovenproof dish.

For the topping, mix the breadcrumbs and melted coconut oil with some salt and pepper and sprinkle evenly over the chicken. Bake for 25 minutes, or until the chicken is cooked through (I use a Thermapen to check; it should read 75°C/167°F in the centre).

4 boneless chicken breasts

FOR THE PESTO
80g/2¾ oz mixed olives
80g/2¾ oz sun-dried tomatoes
1 garlic clove
1 small green chilli (deseeded for
    less heat)
Handful of coriander
50g/1¾ oz gluten-free breadcrumbs
50g/1¾ oz pine nuts, toasted in a
    dry pan
Finely grated zest of 1 lemon

FOR THE TOPPING
60g/2 oz gluten-free breadcrumbs
20g/¾ oz Lucy Bee coconut oil,
    melted
Lucy Bee Himalayan salt and ground
    black pepper

SERVES 4

TIP
If you want to prepare these ahead of time, make them up and freeze after sprinkling over the topping. Defrost thoroughly and then bake.

FETA CHEESE STRAWS

Preheat the oven to 200°C/400°F/gas mark 6. Line
2 baking trays with baking parchment.

Put the flour, xanthan gum, coconut oil and feta into
a food processor and blitz until the mixture resembles
breadcrumbs. Add the egg yolks, water, mustard and
cayenne pepper. Blitz again until it forms a dough. Wrap
the dough in cling film and chill in the fridge for 5 minutes.

Divide the dough in half. Roll out one half on a lightly
floured surface to a rectangle approximately 5mm/
⅕ in thick. Using a sharp knife, mark and then cut into
strips about 15 x 1.5cm/6 x ½ in and, while the strips are
still together, brush the top with beaten egg and sprinkle
generously with black sesame seeds. Using a palette
knife, carefully lift the cheese straws one at a time onto
a baking sheet, spacing them out.

Repeat the process for the other half of dough but
sprinkle with golden sesame seeds instead of black.

Bake in the middle of the oven for 15–20 minutes
or until pale golden brown. Remove from the oven
and transfer the straws to a wire rack to cool.

150g/generous 1 cup gluten-free
    plain (all-purpose) flour, plus
    extra for dusting
¼ tsp xanthan gum
65g/2¼ oz Lucy Bee coconut oil
125g/4½ oz feta
2 egg yolks
3 tbsp cold water
1 tsp Dijon mustard
Pinch of cayenne pepper

TO FINISH
1 egg, beaten
Roasted black sesame seeds and
    golden sesame seeds

MAKES ABOUT 30

BEETROOT AND GOAT'S CHEESE TART

Preheat the oven to 200°C/400°F/gas mark 6. Lightly
grease a 24cm/9 in fluted tart tin with coconut oil.

Roll out the pastry between two sheets of cling film
until very thin and big enough to line the tin. Peel off the
top sheet of cling film and invert the pastry into the tin.
Remove the second sheet of cling film. If the pastry tears,
press it into gaps with your fingers. Neaten the top edge
of the pastry with a knife. Chill in the freezer for 5 minutes.

Line the pastry case with baking parchment and baking
beans and blind bake in the middle of the oven for 10–15
minutes until the pastry just begins to colour. Remove the
beans and parchment and return the pastry to the oven for
a further 5 minutes. Remove from the oven and leave to
cool. Reduce the oven to 180°C/350°F/gas mark 4.

Heat the coconut oil in a frying pan, add the onion and
sauté over a gentle heat until soft.

Using an electric whisk, mix together the eggs, yoghurt,
dill and some salt and pepper. Add the red onion, beetroot
(beets) and goat's cheese to the egg mixture, stir then pour
into the pastry case. Cook in the oven for 25–30 minutes
until set, then serve warm or at room temperature.

1 tbsp Lucy Bee coconut oil, plus
    extra for greasing
1 quantity Gluten-Free Pastry
    (see page 183)
1 red onion, chopped
4 eggs
140g/5 oz Greek yoghurt
5g/⅛ oz fresh dill, finely chopped
250g/8¾ oz cooked beetroot
    (beets), diced
100g/3½ oz soft goat's cheese, cut
    into small dice
Lucy Bee Himalayan salt and ground
    black pepper

SERVES 6

GARDENER'S PIE

My sister came up with the name for this vegan version of a shepherd's pie. It takes a little while to create but is definitely worth the effort. Try keeping your vegetables seasonal!

Preheat the oven to 200°C/400°F/gas mark 6.

Melt the coconut oil in a heavy-based pan, add the sun-dried tomato oil and onions and gently fry until soft, then add the garlic and cook for 1 minute. Add the carrots, parsnips, celery, mushrooms, pepper and sun-dried tomatoes, mix together and cook for a further 5 minutes. Add the lentils and vegetable stock, stir together, taste and season before adding the thyme and rosemary.

Bring to the boil, cover and simmer for 10 minutes. Check the consistency, and if the mixture seems too runny leave the lid off and continue cooking for a further 10 minutes to reduce (if the consistency is fine, continue cooking with lid on for 10 minutes) then remove from the heat. If using fresh thyme and rosemary, discard these at this point. Stir in the chopped parsley.

While the mixture is cooking, steam the potatoes and celeriac in a steamer until soft. Place in bowl and, using an electric whisk, purée to a mash with the mustard and some salt and pepper.

Transfer the vegetable mixture to an ovenproof dish, spread the potato mixture evenly on top and bake in the oven for 20 minutes before serving.

30g/1 oz Lucy Bee coconut oil
80g/¾ cup sun-dried tomatoes from a jar, plus 3 tbsp of the oil
200g/7 oz onions, finely chopped
3 garlic cloves, finely chopped
250g/8¾ oz carrots, peeled and grated
200g/7 oz parsnips, peeled and grated
3 celery sticks, finely chopped
250g/8¾ oz chestnut mushrooms, rinsed and finely chopped
1 red pepper (bell pepper), finely chopped
1 x 400g tin/14 oz green lentils, drained and rinsed
300ml/1¼ cups vegetable stock (see page 176 for homemade) with 3 tbsp tomato purée (paste) added
Few fresh thyme sprigs or 2 tsp dried
1 fresh rosemary sprig or ½ tsp dried
Bunch of fresh parsley, chopped
500g/1lb 1 oz potatoes, peeled and cut into chunks
500g/1lb 1 oz celeriac, peeled and cut into chunks
2 tbsp wholegrain mustard
Lucy Bee Himalayan salt and ground black pepper

SERVES 4–6

GF WF LF DF V VEG

WILD MUSHROOM PASTA BAKE

Maybe not one of our healthiest of dishes but a definite comfort food that I love to tuck in to. Try it with your favourite pasta shape – mine is penne.

Preheat the oven to 180°C/350°F/gas mark 4.

Cook the pasta according to the instructions on the packet, drain, rinse in cold water to stop it from cooking further, and set aside.

Melt the coconut oil in a deep frying pan over a medium heat. Add the garlic and sauté for 1 minute, then add the mushrooms and continue to cook for 6 minutes, adding the pine nuts after 5 minutes. Stir well, remove from the heat and set aside.

For the sauce, put the coconut oil, flour and milk in a saucepan and stir continuously using a balloon whisk until the sauce thickens. Stir in the cheese and mustard and add black pepper to taste.

Tip the drained pasta into a medium-sized oven dish. Add the garlic mushrooms and cheese sauce and mix it all together. Grate a generous layer of Parmesan over the top and bake in the oven for 10 minutes until bubbling and golden. Serve with rocket (arugula).

150g/5¼ oz brown rice pasta
  (I use Rizopia brand)
1 tbsp Lucy Bee coconut oil
3 garlic cloves, finely chopped
300g/10½ oz mixed wild
  mushrooms, such as shiitake,
  oyster or cremini, halved
20g/¾ oz pine nuts
Parmesan, for grating
Rocket (arugula), to serve

FOR THE CHEESE SAUCE
40g/1½ oz Lucy Bee coconut oil
40g/⅓ cup gluten-free plain
  (all-purpose) flour
500ml/2 cups plus 1 tbsp milk
60g/2 oz Cheddar cheese, grated
1 tbsp wholegrain mustard
Ground black pepper

SERVES 2

ROASTED ROOT VEGETABLE PASTA

Filling and soothing, this is great on a cold day and an easy way to get your five-a-day in. Brown rice pasta is one of those carbs that goes with almost anything.

Preheat the oven to 180°C/350°F/gas mark 4.

Melt the coconut oil in a large ovenproof frying pan over a medium heat, then add the sprouts, carrots, parsnips, onions, garlic and aubergines (eggplants), stirring to mix. Cook for 5 minutes, then transfer to the oven for 30 minutes, turning the vegetables halfway through roasting.

Meanwhile, cook the pasta according to the instructions on the packet, then drain and rinse in cold water to prevent the pasta from continuing to cook.

Remove the roasted vegetables from the oven, mix in the pasta, drizzle over a little olive oil, stir in the parsley and add salt and pepper to taste.

To serve, sprinkle with the pine nuts and some grated Parmesan.

50g/1¾ oz Lucy Bee coconut oil
200g/7 oz Brussels sprouts, outer leaves removed, halved
200g/7 oz carrots, peeled and cut into 2cm/¾ in cubes
200g/7 oz parsnips, peeled and cut into 2cm/¾ in cubes
200g/7 oz red onions, peeled and each cut into 8 pieces
2 garlic cloves, crushed
250g/8¾ oz aubergines (eggplants), cut into 2cm/¾ in cubes
300g/10½ oz organic brown rice pasta (I use Rizopia brand)
Extra virgin olive oil, to drizzle
Massive handful of parsley, chopped
Lucy Bee Himalayan salt and ground black pepper

TO SERVE
50g/1¾ oz pine nuts, toasted in a dry pan
Grated Parmesan

SERVES 2–4

TIP
Refresh cooked brown rice pasta by pouring boiling water over it.

ROASTED RED PEPPER PESTO PASTA

Try saying that in a hurry or when you've had a glass of wine! Oh-so easy to make and very satisfying, this is perfect after a busy day on the go.

Preheat the oven to 170°C/325°F/gas mark 3.

For the pesto, add the garlic, lemon juice, basil, pine nuts, Parmesan, roasted red (bell) peppers, sun-dried tomatoes with their oil and olive oil to a food processor and blitz, adding a splash of water if necessary to make it less thick.

Cook the pasta according to the instructions on the packet, then drain, rinse in cold water and mix with the pesto. Tip into a baking tray, top with a little more Parmesan and pine nuts and bake in the oven for 5 minutes. Top with parsley and serve with a refreshing side salad.

400g/14 oz brown rice pasta
   (I use Rizopia brand)
10g/⅓ oz fresh parsley, chopped

FOR THE PESTO
1 garlic clove
Juice of 1 lemon
15g/½ oz fresh basil
30g/1 oz pine nuts, plus extra
   to finish
50g/1¾ oz Parmesan, grated, plus
   extra to finish
120g/4½ oz roasted red (bell)
   peppers from a jar
50g/scant ½ cup sun-dried
   tomatoes from a jar, plus 1 tbsp
   of the oil
3 tbsp extra virgin olive oil

SERVES 4

TIP
If you can't tolerate lactose, this pesto sauce works equally as well using a lactose-free hard cheese.

SPICY PRAWN PASTA

Cook the pasta according to the instructions on the packet, then drain and rinse in cold water to stop it from continuing to cook.

Meanwhile, heat the coconut oil in a frying pan, add the onions and sauté until soft. Add the garlic and chilli flakes and sauté for a further 2 minutes. Add the prawns (shrimp) and cook until they turn pink, then remove from the heat and stir in the parsley.

Stir the prawns and pasta together and drizzle a little extra virgin olive oil over before seasoning. Serve with grated Parmesan, if you like.

150–200g/5¼–7 oz brown rice pasta (I use Rizopia brand)
2 tbsp Lucy Bee coconut oil
150g/5¼ oz red onions, finely chopped
2 garlic cloves, finely chopped
¼ tsp dried chilli flakes (or a pinch if you want it less hot)
200g/7 oz raw prawns (shrimp), peeled and deveined
Big handful of parsley, chopped
Drizzle of extra virgin olive oil
Lucy Bee Himalayan salt and ground black pepper
Grated Parmesan, to serve (optional)

SERVES 2

LIGHT PESTO CHICKEN

Put the garlic, basil, Parmesan, lime juice, olive oil and two thirds of the pine nuts in a food processor and blitz, adding a dash of water if needed to make it less thick.

Heat the coconut oil in a frying pan over a medium-high heat, then add the chicken strips and fry until cooked through, about 7 minutes, turning them halfway.

While the chicken is cooking, peel the carrots and, using a swivel peeler, pare them into strips. Put the chicken and carrots into a bowl and stir in the pesto.

Quickly toast the remaining pine nuts in a dry frying pan, sprinkle over the chicken and enjoy!

2 garlic cloves
20g/¾ oz fresh basil leaves
40g/1½ oz Parmesan
Juice of 2 limes
4 tbsp olive oil
60g/½ cup pine nuts
1 tbsp Lucy Bee coconut oil
2 boneless, skinless chicken breasts, cut into strips
2 large carrots

SERVES 2

SPANISH CHICKEN CASSEROLE

'Buen provecho!' is Spanish for 'bon appetit!'.
That says it all really for this hearty dish.

Preheat the oven to 150°C/300°F/gas mark 2.

Dust the chicken thighs with the paprika. Melt the coconut oil in a large ovenproof frying pan that has a lid, or in a flameproof casserole, then add the chorizo and fry for about 5 minutes, before adding the chicken and browning on each side.

Remove the chicken and chorizo to a dish or plate, add the onions, garlic, fennel and (bell) peppers and fry for 10 minutes over a medium heat, until soft. Add the potato slices and sun-dried tomatoes, and return the chicken and chorizo to the pan.

Pour the sherry or Marsala over then add the tomatoes and stock and mix all the ingredients together. Bring to the boil, cover and cook in the oven for 2 hours, giving it a stir halfway through. Before serving, stir in the parsley and scatter over the olives.

8 chicken thighs on the bone, skin removed
1 tbsp paprika (mild or hot as you prefer)
1 tbsp Lucy Bee coconut oil
50g/1¾ oz chorizo, chopped
200g/7 oz red onions, sliced
2 garlic cloves, chopped
2 fennel bulbs, sliced
2 red peppers (bell peppers), deseeded and sliced
400g/14 oz waxy potatoes, peeled and quartered
100g/scant 1 cup sun-dried tomatoes, halved
75ml/⅓ cup medium or sweet sherry, or Marsala
1 x 400g tin/2 cups chopped tomatoes
500ml/2 cups plus 1 tbsp chicken stock (see page 177 for homemade)
Handful of parsley, chopped
Small handful of olives

SERVES 4

TIP
This dish freezes well.

GF · WF · LF · DF · V · VEG

CHICKEN PIE

What can be better than getting together with family and friends and having a good old catch-up? This pie is made for just that — plonk your masterpiece in the middle of the table along with some vegetables and let everyone help themselves, then sit back and relax.

Preheat the oven to 170°C/325°F/gas mark 3.

Remove the chicken skin and strip the meat from the bones and put into a bowl. (At home we always make stock with the bones. If you don't want to make stock at this stage, you can place the bones in a freezer bag and freeze until later — see the recipe on page 177.)

Heat the coconut oil in a frying pan and sauté the leeks, onion, garlic, tarragon and mushrooms, if using, until soft. Mix this into the chicken.

To make the sauce, put the flour, coconut oil and milk in a saucepan. Stir with a balloon whisk over a medium heat, to avoid any lumps, until thickened, then stir in the mustard and remove from the heat. Stir the sauce into the chicken mixture and add salt and pepper to taste.

Roll out half the pastry on a sheet of cling film to a round big enough to fit into a 24cm/9 in diameter round pie dish. Carefully turn over the cling film (so the cling film is on top) and push the pastry gently into the pie dish. Fill with the chicken mixture. Lightly moisten the edges of the pastry and roll out the remaining pastry, using the same technique. Place over the pie and press the edges together using a fork, to seal, trimming off any excess pastry.

If you like, make a leaf pattern with any leftover pastry (or use to make mini tarts) and brush over with egg yolk.

Bake in the oven for 50–60 minutes, until the pastry is nicely coloured.

PASTRY
500g/1lb 1 oz gluten-free pastry
(for homemade see page 183;
you will need a double quantity)

FILLING
1 whole roasted chicken
1 tbsp Lucy Bee coconut oil
2 large leeks, thinly sliced
1 large onion, chopped
2 garlic cloves, crushed
1 tbsp dried tarragon
125g/4½ oz mushrooms, finely
chopped (optional)
1 egg yolk, lightly beaten

SAUCE
40g/⅓ cup gluten-free plain
(all-purpose) flour
40g/1½ oz Lucy Bee coconut oil
500ml/2 cups plus 1 tbsp milk
1 tbsp Dijon mustard
Lucy Bee Himalayan salt and ground
black pepper

SERVES 4–6

> ## NOTE
> If you prefer your pie to have more sauce, increase the flour quantity to 75g/⅔ cup, the coconut oil to 80g/2½ oz, and the milk to 800ml/scant 3½ cups.

LAMB SHANKS WITH POMEGRANATE MOLASSES

This dish takes a lot longer to cook than most of the other recipes in the book and you'll see why once you taste it. It definitely tastes better the longer you leave it. The combination of pomegranate and lamb is something that your taste buds will love you for.

Preheat the oven to 150°C/300°F/gas mark 2.

Blitz the cumin and coriander seeds in a spice grinder. Blitz the ginger and garlic together in a small food processor (or grate both and crush them together).

Melt the coconut oil in a flameproof casserole and, when hot, add the lamb shanks, season and brown all over, then remove from the casserole and set aside.

Add the onions to the casserole and stir continuously over a medium-low heat until brown on the edges. Add the garlic and ginger mixture and stir for 1 minute, before adding all the spices. Stir to mix, add a little of the stock to prevent the ingredients from sticking, and cook for about 2 minutes.

Add the tomatoes, remainder of the stock, the tomato purée (paste) and pomegranate molasses and mix everything together well.

Place the lamb shanks back in the casserole, coat in the sauce and bring to the boil. Cover with the lid and cook in the oven for 3–4 hours, checking halfway through the cooking and adding a little water if needed. The lamb is ready when it falls off the bone.

Stir in the coriander and sprinkle over with pomegranate seeds to serve.

1 tsp cumin seeds
1 tsp coriander seeds
60g/2 oz fresh ginger, peeled
2 garlic cloves, peeled
1 tbsp Lucy Bee coconut oil
2 lamb shanks
200g/7 oz red onions, chopped
1 tsp Lucy Bee turmeric powder
10 cardamom pods
1 tsp Lucy Bee cinnamon powder
½ tsp dried chilli flakes
400ml/1⅔ cups chicken stock (see page 177 for homemade)
1 x 400g tin/2 cups cherry tomatoes
1 tbsp tomato purée (paste)
2 tbsp pomegranate molasses
Handful of fresh coriander (cilantro), chopped
Lucy Bee Himalayan salt and ground black pepper
Pomegranate seeds, to serve

SERVES 2

STEAK AND GARLIC
IN RED WINE

An all-time favourite and usual choice as a birthday meal with my family. Just make sure you haven't got to be up close and personal with anybody the next day!

Mix the flour with a pinch each of salt and pepper. Dip the steaks in the flour to coat well on each side and set aside.

Melt a little of the coconut oil in a heavy-based pan, add the garlic and fry until golden. Spoon the garlic out of the pan and set aside. Place the pan back over a high heat, add the remaining coconut oil to the pan and, when hot, add the steaks and sear briefly to brown on each side.

Add the wine a little at a time, letting it bubble and evaporate quickly to prevent the steak from stewing, pouring in the next addition when the last has almost evaporated completely and turning the steaks as you go. It's worth being patient with this, or your sauce will be bitter.

Let the final addition of wine bubble down to a thick sauce, then stir in the parsley or chives, add salt and pepper to taste and serve.

40g/⅓ cup gluten-free plain (all-purpose) flour
2 fillet steaks, no thicker than 4cm/1½ in
20g/¾ oz Lucy Bee coconut oil
3 garlic cloves, crushed
200ml/¾ cup plus 1 tbsp good-quality red wine
Handful of parsley or chives, chopped
Lucy Bee Himalayan salt and ground black pepper

SERVES 2

TIP
This is definitely a family favourite served with roast potatoes! I've used fillet steak in this recipe as we love this as a treat, but feel free to use another cut of steak if you prefer.

LOW-CARB LASAGNE

Low-carb never tasted so good. Perfect if you're trying to stay off the carbs but still fancy something warming and don't want to feel like you're missing out.

Preheat the oven to 170°C/325°F/gas mark 3.

Fry the courgette (zucchini) slices on both sides in the coconut oil. Transfer to a plate and set aside.

To make the white sauce, put the coconut oil, cornflour (cornstarch) and milk in a saucepan and stir continuously over a medium heat until it thickens, then stir in the mustard.

To assemble the lasagne, place a layer of bolognese sauce in the base of an ovenproof dish, then a layer of courgettes, followed by a little of the white sauce (you need to save enough sauce to cover the top of the lasagne) and continue layering until the ingredients are used up (I do 3 layers of each), ending with the white sauce covering the top.

Sprinkle with grated Parmesan, if using, and bake in the oven for 45 minutes.

340g/12 oz courgettes (zucchini), ends trimmed and thinly sliced lengthways
A little Lucy Bee coconut oil
1 quantity Bolognese Sauce (see page 131)
Grated Parmesan (optional, for the top)

FOR THE WHITE SAUCE
50g/1¾ oz Lucy Bee coconut oil
50g/½ cup cornflour (cornstarch)
800ml/scant 3½ cups milk
1 tbsp Dijon mustard

SERVES 4

TIP
This dish freezes well. Defrost before baking. Great served with a salad.

ONE POT COOKS

In my eyes, these recipes mean one less thing to wash up, or in fact, only one thing to wash up. They are brilliant for when you get in from work or have limited time, need a shower or are tired from the day you've had, but also want to make a nutritious meal that doesn't take up too much time or effort. All you need to do is chop everything up and throw it all into the same pan or tray and leave it to cook while you get on with whatever needs to be done. I always find these dishes get better over time, so are good for taking to work the next day – from soups, to One-Tray Roast Chicken and even Seafood Stew!

RED PEPPER AND SWEET POTATO SOUP

I can't get enough of sweet potatoes. This is yet another great way to include them in your diet.

Melt the coconut oil in a heavy-based saucepan over a medium heat. Add the onions, sweet potatoes, smoked paprika and garlic and sauté for 5 minutes or until the onions are soft, stirring occasionally.

Add the stock, bring to the boil, then turn down the heat and simmer for 10 minutes or until the sweet potatoes are soft. Add the roasted red (bell) peppers and simmer for a further 5 minutes.

Remove from the heat and leave to stand for 5 minutes before blitzing in a blender or food processor. Drizzle with olive oil and stir in the chopped coriander (cilantro) to serve.

2 tbsp Lucy Bee coconut oil
250g/8¾ oz red onions, chopped
600g/1lb 5 oz sweet potatoes, peeled and chopped
1 tsp smoked paprika (mild or hot as you prefer)
1 garlic clove, crushed
1.2 litres/5 cups vegetable stock (see page 176 for homemade)
1 x 460g/16 oz jar roasted red (bell) peppers, drained and chopped
Drizzle of extra virgin olive oil
Handful of coriander (cilantro), chopped

SERVES 4–6

SPINACH AND PEA SOUP

Go green! Surely you must feel healthier just looking at this soup?

Melt the coconut oil in a heavy-based saucepan, add the onion and fry over a medium heat until just starting to soften, then add the garlic and fry for a further 1 minute.

Add the celeriac and stock, bring to the boil, turn down the heat and simmer, uncovered, for 10–15 minutes until the celeriac is soft. Add the spinach, peas, chilli flakes and salt and pepper to taste and bring to the boil, stirring occasionally. Remove from the heat and leave to stand for 5 minutes before blitzing in a blender or food processor.

Serve with a drizzle of olive oil and toasted pumpkin seeds sprinkled on top.

2 tbsp Lucy Bee coconut oil
1 large onion, chopped
1 large garlic clove, chopped
450g/1 lb celeriac, peeled and cubed
1.5 litres/6⅓ cups vegetable stock (see page 176 for homemade)
250g/8¾ oz spinach leaves, rinsed
500g/4 cups frozen peas
¼ tsp dried chilli flakes, to taste (optional)
Lucy Bee Himalayan salt and ground black pepper
Drizzle of extra virgin olive oil
Toasted pumpkin seeds, to serve

SERVES 2–4

QUICK TOMATO SOUP

A true hug in a bowl, this always reminds me of when I was little and had soup when I was feeling unwell. Finding one that isn't full of sugar and additives isn't always easy so try my clean recipe here and you'll be back on your feet in no time!

Heat the coconut oil in a heavy-based pan. When hot, add the garlic and cook for a minute or two over a medium heat, until golden. Add the chilli and red (bell) pepper and cook until soft.

Add the tomatoes, spinach, basil and lemon juice. Bring to the boil, turn the heat down to low and add Greek yoghurt, if using (it gives the soup a creamy texture).

Season with salt and pepper and serve with a drizzle of extra virgin olive oil and some shredded basil leaves.

1 tbsp Lucy Bee coconut oil
2 garlic cloves, finely chopped
½–1 red chilli, thinly sliced (seeds left in if you prefer it hotter)
1 red pepper (bell pepper), deseeded and chopped
1 x 400g tin/2 cups chopped tomatoes
Large handful of spinach
Handful of basil leaves
Juice of ½ lemon
1 tbsp Greek yoghurt (optional)
Lucy Bee Himalayan salt and ground black pepper

TO SERVE
Extra virgin olive oil
Few basil leaves, shredded

SERVES 2

CHICKEN SOUP

Packed with protein this soup is just the job when you've got a busy afternoon ahead. Great to take to work with you or even to enjoy for a simple dinner. Whether true or not, I always think of the saying 'chicken soup for the soul' — you just know it's good for you.

Melt the coconut oil in a large saucepan, add the onions and garlic and sauté over a low heat until soft. Add all the vegetables and cook, stirring, for about 10 minutes, then add the stock, herbs and some salt and pepper.

Bring to the boil, then turn down the heat to medium-low, so the soup is softly bubbling. Cover and cook for 30 minutes, then add the chicken, peas and sweetcorn. Bring back to the boil and continue cooking for 15 minutes or until the chicken is cooked. Stir in the chopped parsley to serve.

30g/1 oz Lucy Bee coconut oil
200g/7 oz onions, chopped
1 large garlic clove, finely chopped
½ celeriac (about 340g/12 oz), peeled and cut into small cubes
3 celery sticks, finely chopped
1 fennel bulb, chopped
200g/7 oz parsnips, peeled and cut into cubes
300g/10½ oz carrots, diced
1 red and 1 yellow pepper (bell peppers), deseeded and chopped
1.5 litres/6⅓ cups chicken stock (see page 177 for homemade)
Few thyme sprigs
2 bay leaves
1 rosemary sprig
2 boneless, skinless chicken breasts, cubed
100g/⅔ cups frozen peas
100g/¾ cup frozen or tinned sweetcorn
Big handful of parsley, chopped
Lucy Bee Himalayan salt and ground black pepper

SERVES 4–6

TIP
This freezes well. Defrost thoroughly before heating. Serve with gluten-free croutons — lightly fry in coconut oil until crunchy.

BOLOGNESE SAUCE

If you prefer, you can cook this on the hob over
a low heat instead of in the oven for the last 2 hours.
The Bolognese keeps well in the freezer.

Preheat the oven to 140°C/275°F/gas mark 1.

Heat the coconut oil in a heavy-based ovenproof
saucepan or flameproof casserole, then add the garlic,
onions, celery and carrots and sauté over a low heat,
stirring occasionally until softened and lightly coloured.

Tip in the mince and cook, stirring to break it up,
until browned, then stir in the mixed herbs and season
well with salt and pepper. Pour in the red wine, if using,
then increase the heat and cook until all the liquid
has evaporated.

Add the sun-dried tomatoes, tinned tomatoes and
red wine vinegar, then bring to the boil, cover and cook
in the oven for 2 hours until all the flavours have mingled.

30g/1 oz Lucy Bee coconut oil
2 garlic cloves, chopped
200g/7 oz onions, chopped
200g/7 oz celery, diced
200g/7 oz carrots, diced
500g/1lb 1 oz Aberdeen Angus beef
    mince
1 tbsp dried mixed herbs or a sprig
    each of fresh thyme and rosemary
100ml/scant ½ cup red wine
    (optional)
150g/1⅓ cups sun-dried tomatoes,
    finely chopped
2 x 400g tins/4 cups chopped
    tomatoes
1 tbsp red wine vinegar
Lucy Bee Himalayan salt and ground
    black pepper

SERVES 4–6

TIP
This is ideal to make ahead
of time as the flavour really
intensifies. Keep in the fridge
for a couple of days, or freeze.
Defrost thoroughly before
reheating in the oven at
150°C/300°F for 1 hour.

QUINOA
RAINBOW BOWL

This works well if you eat it cold, so it's a good one to throw together in the evening and take to work with you the next day.

Cook the quinoa according to the packet instructions.

Melt the coconut oil in a deep frying pan over a medium-high heat and, when hot, add the chorizo, chilli, yellow and red (bell) pepper and broccoli. Fry for 5 minutes or until cooked to your liking, stirring occasionally.

Turn the heat down to low and add the cooked quinoa, then stir and leave for a few minutes to allow the quinoa to absorb the oil from the chorizo. Season (bearing in mind the chorizo and halloumi are both salty) and stir in the parsley.

Divide the mixture between 2 plates or one big serving dish.

Place the frying pan back over a medium-high heat, add a very small amount of coconut oil and, when hot, place the halloumi slices in the pan and cook for about 2 minutes on each side until turning golden, then place over the quinoa mixture. Mix the lemon juice with the olive oil and drizzle over the halloumi and quinoa to serve.

100g/generous ½ cup quinoa
1 tbsp Lucy Bee coconut oil, plus
    a little extra for the halloumi
60g/2 oz chorizo, chopped
1 green chilli, deseeded and diced
1 yellow pepper (bell pepper),
    deseeded and chopped
1 red pepper (bell pepper), deseeded
    and chopped
6 long-stem broccoli florets, each
    chopped into 3 pieces
Handful of parsley, chopped
100g/3½ oz halloumi, thinly sliced
Juice of 1 lemon
2 tbsp extra virgin olive oil
Lucy Bee Himalayan salt and ground
    black pepper

SERVES 2

ONE-PAN CHICKEN WITH ORANGE, APRICOT AND QUINOA

What I love about this is that you can add it all to the pan and have a deliciously impressive meal with minimal washing up. Leave it to cook while you get on with other bits at home or if you just want to relax, before tucking into a sweet infusion of orange and apricot chicken and quinoa.

Over a medium heat, melt the coconut oil in a large, deep frying pan that has a lid. Add the onions and ginger and sauté until soft.

Add the chicken thighs and cook for 4 minutes, then turn them over and cook for a further 4 minutes, stirring to stop the ingredients from sticking and burning. Remove the chicken to a plate.

Add the almonds, apricots, raisins and cinnamon to the pan. Stir well then add the stock and quinoa, making sure all the ingredients are mixed together. Add the chicken back to the pan and continue cooking until the liquid is gently bubbling, then reduce the heat, cover and simmer gently for 20–30 minutes, until all the liquid has been absorbed, stirring occasionally.

Remove from the heat and stir in the orange zest and juice, parsley and salt and pepper to taste. Leave to stand for 5 minutes before serving with wedges of orange.

1 tbsp Lucy Bee coconut oil
150g/5¼ oz red onions, diced
40g/⅓ cups fresh ginger, peeled and grated
4 boneless, skinless chicken thighs
40g/⅓ cup almonds
60g/2 oz soft dried apricots, quartered
30g/1 oz raisins
½ tsp Lucy Bee cinnamon powder
600ml/2½ cups vegetable stock (see page 176 for homemade)
200g/generous 1 cup quinoa
Finely grated zest and juice of ½ orange (cut the remaining half into wedges to serve)
Big handful of parsley, roughly chopped
Lucy Bee Himalayan salt and ground black pepper

SERVES 2

TURKEY CHILLI WITH CACAO POWDER

This might sound an odd combination at first but believe me it is sooo good! The cacao adds a wonderful richness to the sauce and I even like this cold the following day.

Melt the coconut oil in a heavy-based frying pan over a medium heat. Add the onions and sauté for 2 minutes or until soft, stirring every now and then. Add the garlic and carrots and continue cooking for about 5 minutes, stirring occasionally.

Add the turkey mince and, using a wooden spoon, break up any large lumps. Cook for 5 minutes before adding the cumin seeds, smoked paprika, coriander seeds and chilli flakes.

Make sure everything is thoroughly mixed, then add the tomatoes, tomato purée (paste), cacao powder and black (turtle) beans and stir everything together. Add salt and pepper to taste and bring to the boil, then turn the heat down so the mixture is simmering, cover and cook for 30–40 minutes, stirring occasionally so it doesn't stick to the pan, and adding a little water if the mixture seems to be drying out.

Sprinkle with the chopped coriander (cilantro) and serve with Greek yoghurt.

1 tbsp Lucy Bee coconut oil
2 onions, finely chopped
2 garlic cloves, crushed
2–3 carrots, peeled and grated
500g/1lb 1 oz turkey mince
3 tsp cumin seeds
2 tsp smoked paprika
1 tsp coriander seeds, crushed
½ tsp dried chilli flakes (or 1 tsp if you are feeling brave!)
1 x 400g tin/2 cups chopped tomatoes
1 tbsp tomato purée (paste)
1 tbsp Lucy Bee cacao powder
1 x 400g tin/1⅔ cups black (turtle) beans, drained and rinsed
Handful of coriander (cilantro), chopped
Lucy Bee Himalayan salt and ground black pepper
Greek yoghurt, to serve

SERVES 6

SEAFOOD STEW

This dish really makes me feel as though I'm on holiday and it's great to have with your favourite glass of wine. My top tip for this would be to visit your local fishmonger, or ask at the fish counter in your supermarket, and see what fish they have in. It's easy to substitute our suggestions with whatever you buy.

Melt the coconut oil in a deep pan over a medium heat, add the onion and garlic and sauté until golden, then set aside.

Put the (bell) pepper, celery, olive oil, lemon juice, paprika and cayenne pepper into a food processor and blitz together to form a chunky paste. Add the paste to the pan and cook over a medium heat, stirring continuously.

Add the tomatoes, stir, then add the white fish, prawns (shrimp) and mussels. Season to taste, cover and simmer for 10 minutes. Sprinkle with parsley and serve hot, with a wedge of your favourite homemade bread.

1 tsp Lucy Bee coconut oil
1 medium red onion, chopped
3 garlic cloves, chopped
1 red pepper (bell pepper), deseeded and chopped (or for sweetness use red peppers from a jar)
2 celery sticks, chopped
2 tbsp virgin olive oil
Juice of ½ lemon
1 tsp paprika
½ tsp cayenne pepper
1 x 400g/14 oz tin tomatoes
400g/14 oz white fish, such as haddock or cod, cut into small chunks
140g/5 oz raw prawns (shrimp), peeled and deveined
200g/7 oz mussels in shells, scrubbed and de-bearded
Lucy Bee Himalayan salt and ground black pepper
Handful of parsley, chopped, to serve

SERVES 4

ONE-TRAY ROAST CHICKEN

Who normally ends up doing all the washing up after a marathon of cooking and using every gadget, pot and pan for a roast? Well, if it's normally you, great news... This uses just one tray, yet is still very impressive if you have guests over!

Preheat the oven to 180°C/350°F/gas mark 4.

For the marinade, put the lemon zest, garlic, thyme, rosemary and melted coconut oil in a bowl and mix together. Set aside while you prepare the chicken.

Place the chicken in a large baking tray and push 4 lemon quarters and 4 onion quarters, the thyme and the rosemary into the cavity. Add the remaining lemon and onion to the tray with the carrots, parsnips and potatoes, with salt and pepper to taste. Pour the marinade over the chicken and vegetables, making sure it is evenly distributed.

Cover the chicken but not the vegetables with foil and cook in the oven for 1 hour, then remove the foil and continue roasting until the chicken is cooked (according to the cooking time calculated from its weight; check by piercing between the leg and body with a sharp knife or skewer, and the juices should run clear). Remove the chicken to a board and leave to rest for 15 minutes before carving, returning the vegetables to the oven in the meantime to finsih cooking.

1 large chicken
2 large onions, peeled and quartered
2 large lemons, quartered
Handful of fresh thyme
Handful of fresh rosemary
4 large carrots, peeled and quartered
4 parsnips, peeled and quartered
2 large potatoes, peeled and quartered
Lucy Bee Himalayan salt and ground black pepper

FOR THE MARINADE

Grated zest of 1 large lemon
4 garlic cloves, crushed
Few thyme leaves
Few rosemary leaves
50g/1¾ oz Lucy Bee coconut oil, melted

SERVES 4

NAUGHTY
BUT NICE

It's key for us to have a balanced diet, and you'll have heard us say 'everything in moderation' before...
Or, eat the whole dessert and worry about moderation afterwards! We have really tried to make these as healthy as possible while still giving you a mouth-watering treat. Some are super simple, like our Salted Caramel Fudge, or a happy medium like Rum and Raisin Cake, or more challenging, but still not too hard, like our gluten-free, dairy-free Profiteroles.

POPCORN

Who doesn't love popcorn? The only reason I used to go to the cinema was so I had an excuse to eat a bucket-load of popcorn and sweets with no guilt. This popcorn is great as a snack at work or hanging with friends, or when you just want a little 'you' time.

Melt the coconut oil in a large saucepan over a medium heat. Add the corn and put the lid on – otherwise the corn will jump out! Cook for 4–5 minutes, until you can hear that the corn has finished popping. Sprinkle over your topping of choice and serve.

1 tsp Lucy Bee coconut oil
50g/⅓ cup popping corn

TOPPING OPTIONS
20g/¾ oz desiccated coconut chips
20g/¾ oz raisins
Drizzle of maple syrup
1 tsp Lucy Bee cinnamon powder
1 tsp Lucy Bee Himalayan salt

SERVES 1

CACAO AND CINNAMON BALLS

These really are little balls of heaven!

Put all the ingredients into a food processor and blitz together until they resemble a crumble mixture. Leave to stand in the fridge for 5 minutes, before forming into balls.

Store in the fridge or freezer. These will keep for a couple of weeks (if you haven't eaten them all by then!).

75g/¾ oz gluten-free porridge oats
75g/½ cup almonds
180g/6¼ oz dates, stones removed
75g/2¾ oz dried figs
3 tbsp Lucy Bee cinnamon powder
3 tbsp Lucy Bee maca powder
50g/1¾ oz cacao butter
30g/1 oz Lucy Bee coconut oil

MAKES ABOUT 20

GINGER AND MACA BALLS

Being healthy just got a little spicier.

Put the cashew nuts into a small bowl and add hot water from the kettle to cover. Leave to soak for 2 hours, then drain.

Add all the ingredients except the desiccated coconut to a food processor and blitz until they resemble a crumble mixture. Refrigerate for 5 minutes, then form the mixture into balls and roll each in desiccated coconut to coat.

Store in the fridge or freezer. These will keep for a couple of weeks.

100g/scant 1 cup cashew nuts
50g/⅓ cup pumpkin seeds, toasted
  in a dry pan
180g/6¼ oz dates, stones removed
1½ tbsp ground ginger
2 tbsp Lucy Bee cinnamon powder
2 tbsp Lucy Bee maca powder
50g/1¾ oz coconut butter
30g/1 oz Lucy Bee coconut oil
Desiccated coconut, for coating

MAKES ABOUT 20

SWIRLED CACAO MERINGUES

These meringues look very impressive but are so easy to make, the chocolate twist makes it look like you've really put some thought into the styling of them! #cheatswayofcooking

Preheat the oven to 130°C/250°F/gas mark ½. Line a baking sheet with baking parchment.

Using an electric whisk, whisk the egg whites until they form stiff peaks, then add the sugar, a spoonful at a time, whisking continuously, until you have a lovely glossy meringue. Add in the cornflour (cornstarch) and vinegar and whisk into the mixture.

Sift in the cacao powder and fold it through briefly using a large metal spoon – just two or three folds so that you get a swirled effect.

Spoon the mixture onto the prepared baking sheet, making each meringue about 10cm/4 in in diameter. Bake for about 1 hour, or until they come off easily from the baking parchment. Transfer to a wire rack to cool.

4 medium egg whites, at room temperature
220g/1 cup caster (superfine) sugar
1 tsp cornflour (cornstarch)
1 tsp white wine vinegar or distilled vinegar
2 tbsp Lucy Bee cacao powder

MAKES 8 INDIVIDUAL MERINGUES

CHEWY NUTTY LUCUMA BARS WITH FLAXSEED

Just the job when you get a 4pm sugar craving. These keep in the fridge well, so you won't have an excuse to go for an unhealthy option from the cupboard.

Line a baking tray with baking parchment.

Blend the nuts in a food processor until they are in small pieces, or if you prefer a nuttier texture, until half smooth and half still textured. Put into a bowl and add the lucuma, cinnamon, flaxseed and salt.

Melt the coconut oil in a separate bowl. Add the cashew butter and maple syrup and stir well, so that the ingredients are mixed together. Add the blitzed nuts and stir well, until fully combined.

Spoon the mixture onto the lined baking tray and spread it out. Press gently into an even layer and chill in the fridge for 1 hour before cutting into bars.

These last for a couple of weeks – I find they get better the longer you leave them! Store them in the fridge in a sealed container.

80g/scant 1 cup walnuts
80g/⅔ cup hazelnuts (or any nut of your choice; cashews work well)
40g/1½ Lucy Bee lucuma powder
15g/½ oz Lucy Bee cinnamon powder
70g/½ cup milled flaxseed
Pinch of Lucy Bee Himalayan salt
50g/1¾ oz Lucy Bee coconut oil
160g/5½ oz cashew butter (or any nut butter of your choice; I love hazelnut and peanut butter too)
3 tbsp maple syrup

MAKES 12–15

CACAO PEANUT BITES

A very popular treat with our social media following, we felt it would be rude not to add the recipe to the cookbook!

Put the peanut butter, honey and coconut oil in a bowl and leave at room temperature to soften; this makes them easier to work.

Mix in the oats, flaxseed and cacao powder then roll into bite-sized pieces and place on a baking tray. Freeze until set, then eat them straight from the freezer. You only need a couple to satisfy that sweet craving!

100g/3½ oz crunchy peanut butter
30g/1 oz honey
50g/1¾ oz Lucy Bee coconut oil
75g/¾ oz gluten-free rolled oats
50g/1¾ oz milled flaxseed
15g/½ oz Lucy Bee cacao powder

MAKES ABOUT 12

COCONUT, LUCUMA AND LEMON BITES

These bites are light and really refreshing with a zingy citrus burst to them. Ideal for snacking or taking to work.

Line a baking tray with baking parchment.

Put all the ingredients except the coconut oil in a bowl and mix, then add the melted coconut oil and stir together well.

Tip the mixture onto the lined tray and pat down firmly into an even layer. Leave to set for 1–2 hours before cutting into small squares.

Store them in the fridge in a sealed container.

½ tbsp Lucy Bee lucuma powder
2 tbsp maple syrup
1 tsp Lucy Bee cinnamon powder
Finely grated zest and juice of
    1 lemon
100g/1½ cups desiccated coconut
30g/1 oz flaked almonds (or any
    other nut, chopped into small
    pieces)
50g/1¾ oz Lucy Bee coconut oil,
    melted

MAKES 8–10 SQUARES

SALTED CARAMEL FUDGE

Caramel isn't the friendliest of things for the waistline and if you're lactose or dairy intolerant then it's usually a no-no. So after playing around with some of my most used ingredients I ended up with a pretty good fudge, if I do say so myself. Thank me later!

Line a small baking tray with baking parchment.

Blend together the cashew butter, melted coconut oil, maple syrup, salt and lucuma in a food processor. Spread the mixture evenly onto the tray and place in the freezer for 1 hour.

Put all the ingredients for the chocolate sauce into a mixing bowl, mix together well then set aside until your fudge has hardened. If your sauce is too runny, you can leave it in the fridge for a few minutes to harden slightly.

Cut the frozen fudge into small squares, then drizzle over the chocolate sauce. Keep in the fridge – if there are any left over!

FOR THE FUDGE
240g/8½ oz smooth cashew butter, or nut butter of your choice
40g/1½ oz Lucy Bee coconut oil, melted
6 tbsp maple syrup
½ tsp Lucy Bee Himalayan salt
1 tsp Lucy Bee lucuma powder

FOR THE CHOCOLATE SAUCE
30g/1 oz Lucy Bee coconut oil, melted
2 tbsp honey
½ tsp Lucy Bee Himalayan salt (optional)
2 tbsp Lucy Bee cacao powder

MAKES ABOUT 32 SMALL PIECES

PEANUT AND CHOCOLATE BALLS

Peanut butter and chocolate, a pretty good
combination in my eyes. Make this dairy-free
by choosing a dairy-free chocolate.

Line a greaseproof tray with baking parchment.

In a large mixing bowl, stir the peanut butter and
maple syrup together until combined. Add the puffed
brown rice and salt and stir again to mix. Shape into balls
– either 5 large or more, smaller ones. Place in the fridge.

Put the melted coconut oil and chocolate into a
pan and melt the chocolate over a low heat, stirring
continuously and making sure the chocolate doesn't burn.

Remove the peanut balls from the fridge and, using
two large spoons, dip them into the chocolate one at a
time, covering them completely, then place on the lined
tray. Drizzle any leftover chocolate over the balls (or eat
by the spoon!) Put into the freezer for 15 minutes, then
store in the fridge.

200g/7 oz peanut butter (smooth
or crunchy)
2½ tbsp maple syrup
20g/¾ oz gluten-free puffed
brown rice
¼ teaspoon fine grain Himalayan salt
½ tablespoon coconut oil, melted
100g/3½ oz dairy-free dark
chocolate (85% cocoa solids, or
any chocolate of your choice)

MAKES 5 LARGE BALLS

TIP
These are quite rich so you
only need one (or even half)
to satisfy that sweet tooth.

GF WF LF DF V VEG

HIMALAYAN SALTED CARAMEL BITES WITH DATES

These little bites really don't need an introduction, as the name says it all. You're sure to fall in love with these gems of salted caramel goodness.

Line a tray with baking parchment. Place all the ingredients in a food processor and blitz until thoroughly mixed. Roll into small, bite-sized balls, place on the lined tray and chill in the fridge or freezer.

Store in the freezer in an airtight container (they are best eaten straight from the freezer).

100g/3½ oz pitted dates
50g/1¾ oz cashew nuts
30g/1 oz raisins
1 tbsp Lucy Bee coconut oil
2 tbsp ground almonds
2 tbsp maple syrup
½ tsp Lucy Bee Himalayan salt

MAKES 15–20

TIP
These are a good source of natural sugars when you need a pick-me-up.

GF WF LF DF V VEG

ST CLEMENT'S TART

'Just one slice' won't be happening where this tart is involved. A real treat to impress friends with.

Preheat the oven to 200°C/400°F/gas mark 6.

Put the coconut oil, flour, icing (confectioners') sugar, xanthan gum and orange and lemon zests in a food processor and blitz until the mixture resembles breadcrumbs. Add the egg yolks and cold water and blitz again until the mixture comes together and forms a dough. Briefly mould the pastry into a round, wrap in cling film and chill in the fridge for 15 minutes.

Roll out the pastry between 2 sheets of cling film so it is very thin and big enough to line a 23cm/9in loose-based fluted tart tin. Peel off the top sheet of cling film, carefully invert the pastry into the tart tin and remove the second sheet of cling film. If the pastry tears, mould it into gaps with your fingers. Neaten off the top edge of the pastry with a knife and place in the freezer to chill for 5 minutes.

Remove the pastry case from the freezer, line with baking parchment and ceramic baking beans and blind bake in the middle of the oven for 10–15 minutes until the pastry just begins to colour. Remove the baking beans and parchment and return to the oven for a further 5 minutes to cook the base. Remove, set aside to cool and reduce the oven temperature to 150°C/300°F/gas mark 2.

To make the filling, crack the eggs into a large bowl, add the sugar, cream and lemon and orange zest and juice. Using an electric hand-held whisk, beat together until well combined then pour the mixture into a jug.

Pour the filling into the pastry case and carefully place in the oven. Bake for about 20–25 minutes until the filling has just set. Remove from the oven and leave to cool.

Remove the tart from the tin and place on a serving plate. Sift icing sugar over the top and, to glaze, place under a very hot grill to caramelize the icing sugar. Decorate with orange and lemon zest, and serve.

FOR THE PASTRY

90g/3¼ oz Lucy Bee coconut oil (not too hard)
275g/2 cups gluten-free plain (all-purpose) flour
55g/6 tbsp icing (confectioners') sugar
¼ tsp xanthan gum
Finely grated zest of 1 orange
Finely grated zest of 1 lemon
2 egg yolks
3 tbsp cold water

FOR THE FILLING

4 eggs
175g/¾ cup plus 1 tbsp caster (superfine) sugar
150ml/½ cup plus 2 tbsp double (heavy) cream
Finely grated zest and juice of 1 lemon
Finely grated zest and juice of 1 orange
Icing (confectioners') sugar, for dusting
Finely pared strips of orange and lemon zest, to decorate

SERVES 6

APPLE AND GRANOLA TRIFLE

A modern take on a traditional favourite. If you enjoy the granola in this trifle, why not make the quantities bigger and have it for breakfast? My tip if you decide to do this would be to add extra dried fruit for sweetness, rather than too much maple syrup.

Preheat the oven to 150°C/300°F/gas mark 2. Line a small baking tray with baking parchment.

Put the apples and vanilla seeds and pod into a saucepan with the water, bring to the boil, turn down and simmer for 10 minutes, then increase the heat to a bubble to evaporate the water. Take care not to burn the apples at the bottom of the saucepan; keep an eye on it as the water will suddenly evaporate. Remove from the heat and take out the vanilla pod.

While the apples are cooking, put the oats, hazelnuts, walnuts, maple syrup or honey and melted coconut oil in a bowl and mix together, making sure the coconut oil coats all the ingredients. Transfer to the lined tray and bake for 20 minutes until nicely golden, then remove and leave to cool.

Layer the ingredients up in 2 glass tumblers by adding first some granola, then some apple, a thin layer of yoghurt or cream, more apple, some yoghurt or cream, granola to top and a dusting of cinnamon to finish, if you like.

4 crisp dessert apples, such as Granny Smith, peeled and cut into small bite-sized pieces
1 vanilla pod, split lengthways and seeds scraped out
100ml/scant ½ cup water
4 tbsp Greek yoghurt or double (heavy) cream
Lucy Bee cinnamon powder, to taste (optional)

FOR THE GRANOLA
60g/⅔ cup gluten-free oats
40g/1½ oz roasted chopped hazelnuts
20g/¾ oz walnuts, broken into pieces
2 tbsp maple syrup or honey
20g/¾ oz Lucy Bee coconut oil, melted

SERVES 2

APPLE PIE

This is great for a Sunday afternoon, after a roast dinner.
Easy to throw together, it also works well with pear,
too, either mixed half and half with apple or switch
the apple for pear altogether (making it a pear pie!).

Lightly grease a 20 x 20cm/8 x 8 in pie dish with
coconut oil.

Put the coconut oil and flour in a food processor and
pulse until you have a crumbly mix. Add the cold water,
honey and salt and mix until combined. Lightly press the
dough into a ball, wrap it in cling film and refrigerate for
30 minutes.

While the dough is chilling, mix together the apples,
lemon juice, cinnamon and raisins. Preheat the oven to
200°C/400°F/gas mark 6.

Wipe a wet cloth over the kitchen surface and cover
it with a piece of cling film; this will help it to stick to
the surface and help lift the pastry onto the dish. Dust
the cling film with gluten-free flour, unwrap the chilled
dough and place it on the piece of cling film. Flour the
top of the pastry ball and gently roll it out so it is very
thin and big enough to cover the dish.

Fill the pie dish with the apple mixture, lift the cling
film with the pastry on top and invert it over the pie dish,
covering the surface, then peel off the cling film. Use a
fork to press it down on the edges of the pie to seal. It's
always fun to decorate the top with any leftover pieces
of pastry, if you like.

Brush the pastry all over with the beaten egg and
bake in the oven for 10 minutes, then reduce the oven
temperature to 170°C/325°F/gas mark 3 and bake for a
further 25 minutes until golden on top.

FOR THE PASTRY

100g/3½ oz Lucy Bee coconut oil
(solid), plus extra for greasing
180g/1⅓ cups gluten-free plain
(all-purpose) flour, plus extra
for dusting
75ml/⅓ cup ice-cold water
½ tbsp honey
¼ tsp Lucy Bee Himalayan salt
1 egg, beaten

FOR THE FILLING

6 crisp, sweet dessert apples, such
as Pink Lady, cut into small dice
(unpeeled for extra nutrients)
Juice of 1½ lemons
2½ tsp Lucy Bee cinnamon powder
Handful of raisins

SERVES 4–6

RUM AND RAISIN CAKE

This cake tastes better over time, the only problem is, when rum and cake are in the same recipe, I find it hard not to eat the whole lot!

Soak the raisins in the rum for at least 2 hours, or overnight.

Preheat the oven to 180°C/350°F/gas mark 4. Line a 23cm/9 in round cake tin.

Put the melted coconut oil, sugar, eggs, flour, bananas and rum-soaked raisins with any rum not absorbed into a large bowl and, using an electric whisk, mix together. Stir in the pecans and pour the mixture into the lined tin.

Bake for about 50 minutes, until a skewer inserted into the middle of the cake comes out clean, then leave to cool in the tin for a couple of minutes before turning out onto a wire rack to cool.

Store in an airtight container for a couple of days.

50g/1¾ oz raisins
100ml/scant ½ cup spiced dark rum
70g/2½ oz Lucy Bee coconut oil,
 melted
50g/¼ cup light brown sugar
2 medium eggs
275g/2 cups gluten-free
 self-raising flour
2 ripe bananas, roughly chopped
50g/1¾ oz pecans, chopped

SERVES 6

TIP
This loaf cake could be thickly sliced and toasted. Serve with your favourite warm drink.

APRICOT CRUMBLE CAKES

As it says in the name, these cakes really will crumble, so make sure you put one onto a plate before eating or you won't be too popular leaving crumbs all over the house!

Preheat the oven to 170°C/325°F/gas mark 3.

Put the melted coconut oil into a bowl with the oats, flour and honey, and stir together well.

Put the apricots, cranberries, orange zest and juice in a pan and simmer over a medium heat until the apricots soften.

Put a small amount of the oat mixture into each case of a 6-hole silicon muffin tray (or use a regular tray with paper cases), then divide the apricot and cranberry mixture between each. Cover the fruit with the remaining oat mixture (you only need a thin, even layer) and push down gently.

Bake for 20 minutes, then allow to cool before serving. Enjoy with Greek yoghurt.

90g/3¼ oz Lucy Bee coconut oil, melted
120g/1¼ cups gluten-free oats
140g/1 cup plus 1 tbsp gluten-free self-raising flour
4 tbsp honey
100g/3½ oz soft dried apricots, very finely chopped
40g/1½ oz cranberries
Finely grated zest and juice of 1 large orange

MAKES 6

TIP
Best eaten on the day you make them. A popular one with the kids.

DAIRY-FREE
BANOFFEE PIE

Banoffee pie is an English dessert with lots of cream, toffee and condensed milk. Have I lost all the dairy and lactose intolerant people out there? I hope not, as this is dairy-free, using dates and coconut cream instead.

To make the biscuit base, put the ground nuts, dates and coconut oil in a food processor or blender and pulse until combined. Tip into a 24cm/9½-inch loose-based tart tin and press it down with a spoon so it is nice and compact and the whole base and sides are covered. Chill in the fridge for at least 1 hour.

For the caramel, put the dates, water, melted coconut oil and salt into a large, wide saucepan and heat for 15–20 minutes until the dates have softened and the water has almost evaporated. Transfer the mixture to a food processor and blitz until smooth, then leave to cool completely.

For the topping, take the chilled coconut cream out of the fridge and drain off any liquid (you only want to use the thick cream, or it will be too runny). Whip the coconut cream with the icing (confectioners') sugar.

To assemble, push the biscuit base out of the tin onto a flat plate and remove the base of the tin. Smooth the date caramel over the base, add a layer of sliced bananas (save some for the top) then smooth the whipped coconut cream over the bananas. Top with the remaining banana slices and sprinkle with cacao nibs or dark chocolate flakes to decorate.

FOR THE BASE
240g/8½ oz ground nuts of your choice (we used 70g/2½ oz each of cashews and almonds and 100g/3½ oz pecans)
150g/5¼ oz dates
1 tbsp Lucy Bee coconut oil, melted

FOR THE DATE CARAMEL
350g/12½ oz stoned dates
8 tbsp water
2 tbsp Lucy Bee coconut oil, melted
¼ tsp Lucy Bee Himalayan salt

FOR THE TOPPING
320ml/1¼ cups coconut cream (thick coconut milk), refrigerated overnight
1½ tbsp icing (confectioners') sugar
3 bananas, thinly sliced
Cacao nibs or dairy-free dark chocolate flakes, to decorate

SERVES 12

TIP
Make sure the liquid (if any) in the coconut cream is poured off, otherwise the cream will be hard to whip.

GF WF LF DF V VEG

VEGAN CHOCOLATE CAKE

A vegan chocolate cake that is utterly delicious and beautiful to look at. I feel this is going to be a very popular recipe!

Preheat the oven to 150°C/300°F/gas mark 2. Grease and line two 20cm/8 in cake tins.

Combine the dry ingredients in a mixing bowl. In a food processor, purée the bananas and apple together until smooth then transfer to a second bowl. Add the melted coconut oil, vanilla and yoghurt to the purée. Mix together, add to the dry ingredients and mix until well combined.

Slowly add the hot water, while stirring the mixture. Once combined, pour into the prepared tins and bake for 40 minutes, until a skewer inserted into the middle of one comes out clean. Leave to cool in the tins for 5 minutes before turning out onto a wire rack to cool completely.

To make the filling and topping, put the coconut cream into a bowl with the vanilla and icing (confectioners') sugar and, using an electric hand-held mixer, whip until combined. Store in the fridge until the cake is completely cool.

Smooth half the coconut cream over one cake, top with half the berries and place the second cake on top. Spread the remaining coconut cream on top and add the remaining berries. Finally, sift a light dusting of icing sugar over the top and serve.

100g/3½ oz Lucy Bee coconut oil, melted, plus extra for greasing
200g/1½ cups gluten-free plain (all-purpose) flour
100g/½ cup coconut sugar
85g/⅔ cup Lucy Bee cacao powder
1 tsp gluten-free baking powder
2 tsp bicarbonate of soda
2 bananas
1 apple, peeled and cored
1 tsp vanilla extract
200g/7 oz coconut yoghurt, or vegan yoghurt of your choice
220ml/scant 1 cup hot water from the kettle

FOR THE FILLING AND TOPPING
320ml/1¼ cups coconut cream (thick coconut milk), refrigerated
½ tsp vanilla extract
1 tbsp icing (confectioners') sugar, plus extra for dusting
200g/1½ cups blackberries, strawberries and raspberries, or other berries of your choice

SERVES 10

PROFITEROLES

Is it really possible to have dairy-free and gluten-free profiteroles and also keep them pretty healthy, I hear you ask? Well believe me this is just the case here — these have to be a real favourite of mine.

Preheat the oven to 200°C/400°F/gas mark 6. Bring the water to the boil in a saucepan, add the coconut oil and heat just until melted. Turn the heat down to as low as possible, add the flour and mix well using a wooden spoon, stirring until it combines into a ball and has a spongy texture. Take the pan off the heat and leave to cool for 10 minutes.

Add 1 egg to the cooled mixture (it is important it is not hot or the eggs will scramble) and, using an electric hand-held mixer, mix until combined, then mix in the second egg. Keep mixing until smooth, with a pipeable consistency. Spoon the choux mixture into a piping bag and cut a hole at the end about 2cm/¾ inch wide.

Line a baking tray with baking parchment. Pipe the mixture into rounds about 5cm/2 inches across, leaving a 5cm/2-inch space in between each to allow room for them to expand as they cook.

Bake in the oven for 18–20 minutes until golden brown. Remove from the oven and prick each profiterole base with a toothpick, wiggling it around to let the hot air out (this will stop them from going soggy inside). Leave to cool completely on a wire rack.

For the cream filling, put the chilled coconut cream in a bowl and whip to soft peaks, using an electric hand-held mixer. Add the icing (confectioners') sugar and vanilla paste and continue to whip until stiff enough to pipe. Fill a piping bag with the coconut cream mixture and pipe equal amounts inside each profiterole, using the holes you made.

For the chocolate glaze, gently melt the chocolate and coconut oil in a saucepan until smooth, with the consistency of a sauce. Pile the profiteroles into a pyramid and pour the chocolate glaze over the top. They can be stored in the fridge until needed.

FOR THE CHOUX PASTRY
150ml/½ cup plus 2 tbsp water
50g/1¾ oz Lucy Bee coconut oil
85g/1¾ cups gluten-free plain flour
2 eggs

FOR THE CREAM FILLING
160ml/²⁄₃ cup coconut cream (thick coconut milk), refrigerated overnight
1 tsp icing (confectioners') sugar
½ tsp vanilla bean paste

FOR THE CHOCOLATE GLAZE
45g/1½ oz dark dairy-free chocolate (at least 70% cocoa solids), broken into pieces
½ tbsp Lucy Bee coconut oil

MAKES 16

SALTED CARAMEL MOLTEN CAKE WITH CACAO

Wow, this jaw-dropping recipe will impress even the hardest of judges! Unless they don't like salted caramel, then you may have a slight problem...

Preheat the oven to 160°C/320°F/gas mark 3.

In a heatproof bowl set over a pan of simmering water, melt the butter and chocolate together then remove from the heat.

Put the whole egg and yolk with the sugar into a mixing bowl and, using an electric whisk, whisk together until pale. Fold this into the melted chocolate and butter mixture, sift in the flour and cacao and stir well to mix.

Grease 2 ramekin dishes with butter and dust with cacao. Leave to set in the fridge for 2 minutes. Divide the cake mixture between the ramekins and bake for 12–14 minutes –the middle should still be slightly gooey.

Add a dusting of icing (confectioners') sugar and serve straight away, with fresh raspberries if you like.

60g/2 oz butter, plus extra for greasing
60g/2 oz salted caramel dark chocolate
1 whole egg plus 1 yolk
40g/3¼ tbsp coconut sugar
60g/scant ½ cup gluten-free self-raising flour
1 tbsp Lucy Bee cacao powder, plus extra for dusting
Icing (confectioners') sugar, to finish

SERVES 2

LUCY'S LARDER

You'll find here a collection of our must-haves,
from stocks, sauces, mayonnaise and ketchup to a
Sweet Chilli Dipping Sauce and Smoked Salmon Pâté.
Try these and you'll wonder why you bought the
readymade ones for so long!

WHITE SAUCE

Fuss-free white sauce. This sums up my favourite style of cooking: throw everything into one pot and stir!

VEGETABLE STOCK

Making your own stock is surprisingly easy and is really worth the effort, plus you're in control of the amount of salt you add. Whenever I make stock, I always feel so proud of myself!

MAKES ABOUT 550ML/2 CUPS

40g/1½ oz Lucy Bee coconut oil
40g/⅓ cup gluten-free plain (all-purpose) flour
500ml/2 cups plus 1 tbsp milk

Place all the ingredients in a large saucepan. Over a medium heat, use a balloon whisk to whisk continuously for about 8 minutes, when the sauce will start to thicken. Continue cooking and whisking for a further 2 minutes until the sauce thickens.

MAKES ABOUT 2 LITRES/8 CUPS

1 tsp Lucy Bee coconut oil
2 celery sticks, chopped
2 carrots, peeled and chopped
2 onions, chopped
1 leek, chopped
1 garlic clove, crushed (optional)
6 chestnut mushrooms, washed and chopped (optional)
10 whole black peppercorns
3 bay leaves, torn
Few fresh thyme sprigs
Few parsley stalks
1.5 litres/6⅓ cups water

Melt the coconut oil in a large, heavy-based pan over a medium heat. Add the celery, carrots, onions, leek, garlic and mushrooms, if using, and sauté for 2–3 minutes.

Add the peppercorns, bay leaves, thyme, parsley stalks and water and bring to the boil, then cover and simmer gently for 30 minutes.

Allow to cool a little then strain into a bowl or jug. Discard the vegetables and pour the stock into storage or freezer containers (I tend to store this in batches of 500ml/2 cups so it's ready to use in a recipe). Store in the fridge for 2 days or freeze.

> **NOTE**
> Don't worry if you don't have all these ingredients, as you can mix and match with what you have. I sometimes leave out the mushrooms for a clearer stock, and fennel is good to add if you have any in the fridge.
>
> You can also add spices to your stock such as star anise, ginger or lemongrass, which we use in our Ginger Pork Balls in Broth (see page 96). Be adventurous and add your favourite spice!

> **NOTE**
> You can use lactose-free milk or even almond milk to make a lactose-free version of this sauce.

 GF WF LF DF V VEG

 GF WF LF DF V VEG

CHICKEN STOCK

My homemade chicken stock is the perfect base for soups, sauces or gravies. I like to make up huge batches of it and then freeze it in individual portions. Believe me, nothing tastes as nutritious and healthy as your own stock! Star anise makes a wonderful addition to a stock that will be used in an Asian dish.

MAKES ABOUT 1 LITRE/4 CUPS

1kg/2lb 1 oz chicken bones/
    carcasses
2 onions, finely chopped
4 carrots, finely chopped
2 celery sticks, finely chopped
2 garlic cloves, finely chopped
About 12 peppercorns
2 or 3 cloves
2 dried or fresh bay leaves
Few fresh or dried thyme sprigs
Few parsley stalks

Put the chicken bones in a large saucepan or stockpot. Add all the chopped vegetables and cover with cold water. Bring to the boil, skimming off any scum using a spoon.

Add the peppercorns, cloves, bay, thyme and parsley, then cover and cook at a gentle simmer for a couple of hours (or longer, if you wish). Once the bones have fallen apart, strain the stock through a sieve into another saucepan or container.

Leave to stand and beginning to cool before using kitchen paper laid on the surface to remove the fat. If you wish, reduce the stock over a high heat to make it stronger. Portion into the amounts required and freeze when cool.

NOTE

I try to use bones from organic chickens wherever possible. When you cook chickens or joints, always save and freeze the bones and any bits and pieces so that you can use them for stock. Another tip is to save and freeze the stalks from parsley, too, to use in this recipe.

CURRY POWDER

It's so easy to pick up a pre-made curry powder of some sort in the supermarket but if you have a look at the spices you've already got and have a play around with them, you'll be amazed at what you can come up with yourself.

MAKES 2–3 TBSP

1 tsp cumin seeds
1 tsp coriander seeds
1 tsp mustard seeds
1 tsp fenugreek seeds
1 tsp cardamom seeds
    (from the pods)
1 tsp ground ginger
1 tsp Lucy Bee turmeric powder
½–1 tsp chilli powder, depending
    on how much heat you want

Put the cumin, coriander, mustard, fenugreek and cardamom seeds into a heavy-based dry frying pan and warm over a low heat for 1 minute. You should start to notice a wonderful, fragrant smell.

Remove from the heat and leave to cool, then transfer the seeds to a spice grinder and blitz to a powder. Add the ground ginger, turmeric and chilli powder to taste and blitz once more until combined. Store in a Lucy Bee jar.

BEETROOT AND BRAZIL NUT DIP

This vibrant dip is great with celery, cucumber, rice cakes and even works well as a side dish.

SERVES 4–6
300g/10½ oz cooked beetroot
50ml/scant ¼ cup water
80g/2¾ oz Brazil nuts
2 tbsp olive oil
1 tsp balsamic vinegar
Juice of ½ lime
Handful of dill, chopped

Add all ingredients except the dill to a food processor or blender, and blitz. Top with dill and serve.

FETA AND CORIANDER DIP

Coriander leaves its own mark on this flavoursome dip. This is a great one to snack on.

SERVES 4–6
Handful of coriander (cilantro), finely chopped
70g/2½ oz feta, crumbled
1 carrot, grated
100g/3½ oz Greek yoghurt

Mix all ingredients in a bowl and serve.

OLIVE AND ANCHOVY DIP

I love experimenting with flavours and textures to add variety to dips. Try stirring this one into a salad.

SERVES 4–6
100g/1 cup pitted green olives, halved
3 anchovy fillets (in oil)
Juice of ½ lemon
100g/3½ oz Greek yoghurt
Handful of parsley, chopped
1 tbsp olive oil

Add all ingredients to a food processor or blender, and blitz.

BABA GANOUSH (AUBERGINE DIP)

This is a delicious Middle Eastern dip and there are lots of variations on how best to prepare it. Well, of course we think this one is the ultimate in baba ganoush!

SERVES 4

3 medium aubergines (eggplants)
2 tbsp tahini
1 garlic clove, crushed
4 tbsp freshly squeezed
   lemon juice
3 tbsp chopped parsley
1 tbsp extra virgin olive oil
Lucy Bee Himalayan salt and
   ground black pepper

Preheat the oven to 180°C/350°F/gas mark 4.

Preheat the grill to medium and place the whole aubergines (eggplants) on a foil-lined baking tray. With a fork, prick holes all around each aubergine, then grill until the skin starts to blacken and blister, and smell smoky (this adds a lovely flavour to the dip), turning them to grill evenly all over.

Transfer to the oven and bake for 25–30 minutes until very soft. Remove and allow to cool for 15 minutes, then slice the aubergines open and scoop out all the insides into a bowl. Add the remaining ingredients with salt and pepper to taste, adjusting each if necessary and, using a spoon or fork, mash together and stir.

Cover and store in the fridge for up to 3 days.

         GF WF LF DF V VEG

SMOKED SALMON PÂTÉ

Get in your healthy fats with this pâté. Great on its own, with gluten-free bread, rice cakes or even with avocado for breakfast!

SERVES 8

150g/5¼ oz smoked salmon,
   cut into pieces
180g/6¼ oz Greek yoghurt
50g/1¾ oz Lucy Bee coconut oil
Juice of 1 lemon
Pinch of cayenne pepper
Small handful of fresh dill,
   chopped
Lucy Bee Himalayan salt and
   ground black pepper

Add the smoked salmon pieces, yoghurt and coconut oil to a blender and blitz until smooth. Transfer to a bowl and stir in the lemon juice, cayenne pepper and dill. Season to taste, cover with cling film and chill for 30 minutes.

Remove from the fridge approximately 40 minutes before serving. It can be made 2 days ahead and kept in the fridge.

     GF WF LF DF V VEG

AVOCADO AND PEA DIP

This is our twist on a traditional guacamole. It works as a great accompaniment to our Chicken Burger (page 64).

SERVES 4–6

1 large avocado, mashed
100g/3½ oz cooked peas
Juice of 1 lemon
1 large tomato, finely diced
1 tsp olive oil
Lucy Bee Himalayan salt and
   ground black pepper

Mix all the ingredients together with salt and pepper to taste. Cover and store in the fridge for up to 2 days.

      GF WF LF DF V VEG

GARLIC MAYONNAISE

Homemade mayo can be quite tricky to get just right but we've finally conquered it! This mayo is a real hit in our house and has a much cleaner taste than any shop-bought mayo we've tried. It will keep in the fridge for up to 5 days.

**MAKES ENOUGH FOR
5–6 SERVINGS**
1 small garlic clove, peeled
Big pinch of Lucy Bee Himalayan salt
1 egg yolk
1 tbsp apple cider vinegar
1 tbsp Dijon mustard
Up to 140ml/½ cup plus 1 tbsp sunflower oil
60ml/¼ cup extra virgin olive oil

By hand:
Make sure all the ingredients are at room temperature. Beat the egg yolk in a bowl for a couple of minutes, using a balloon whisk or hand-held blender. Add the salt and beat again until thick and sticky. Slowly add the sunflower oil, little by little, starting with a few drops at a time, whisking continuously with the balloon whisk. Take your time here or it might split. Once it has reached the consistency you want, slowly whisk in the olive oil. Once it is all incorporated, give it a good whisk for about 30 seconds until thick and glossy. Mix in the vinegar, mustard and garlic. Your mayo should have a creamy consistency.

**Alternative method using a
Tefal Infiny Force gadget:**
Crush the garlic clove with the salt in a pestle and mortar or using a fork, then put into the small Tefal Infiny Force beaker. Add the egg yolk, vinegar, mustard and enough sunflower oil to reach the mark reading 'min 140ml' on the beaker, topping up to the 'max 200ml' mark, but no higher, with the olive oil. Place the Infiny blender in the base of the jug, making sure it is over the egg yolk, and beat for 5 seconds on turbo then for a further 5 seconds while moving the blender up and down. That's it!

HOMEMADE TOMATO KETCHUP

I'm guilty of enjoying the occasional ketchup overload when eating chips, chicken, burgers or anything that's acceptable to have ketchup with. Store-bought ones can be full of sugars though, so here's a healthier option.

MAKES ABOUT 250ML/1 CUP
1 tsp Lucy Bee coconut oil
1 red onion, sliced
2 garlic cloves, chopped
60ml/¼ cup red wine vinegar
40ml/2 tbsp plus 2 tsp apple cider vinegar
30g/2½ tbsp coconut sugar
Pinch of Lucy Bee Himalayan salt
2 tbsp tomato purée (paste)
1 tsp dried oregano
1 x 400g tin/2 cups chopped tomatoes

Heat the coconut oil in a medium pan over a medium heat, add the onion and cook for 2 minutes, then add the garlic and cook until golden and the onion is soft.

Add both vinegars, the sugar and salt and bring to the boil, stirring continuously. Add the tomato purée (paste), oregano and tinned tomatoes and cook for 15–18 minutes over a medium heat until the sauce reduces and thickens. Allow to cool then process in a blender until smooth. Store in the fridge for up to 3 days.

GF WF LF DF V VEG   GF WF LF DF V VEG

FENNEL AND RED CABBAGE COLESLAW

A very healthy alternative to the normal coleslaw. I usually make this as a side, or have it in a sweet potato jacket. Be warned though if you're anything like me, it's easy to eat it all up before the jacket is even ready.

SERVES 2–4

½ small red cabbage
1 fennel bulb
1 red onion, outer tough skin removed
2 carrots
80g/generous ½ cup pumpkin seeds, toasted in a dry pan

FOR THE DRESSING

50ml/scant ¼ cup extra virgin olive oil
20ml/1 tbsp plus 1 tsp apple cider vinegar
Juice of 1 lemon
1 garlic clove
1 tsp Dijon mustard
100ml/scant ½ cup Greek yoghurt
Drizzle of honey (optional)
Lucy Bee Himalayan salt and ground black pepper

Using the slicing blade on a food processor, shred the cabbage, fennel and onion. Change the blade to the coarse grater and grate the carrots. Alternatively, finely slice the cabbage, fennel, onion and grate the carrot by hand. Mix everything together in a large bowl.

Blitz together the olive oil, apple cider vinegar, lemon juice, garlic and mustard, then whisk in the yoghurt, taste and, if needed, add a little honey to sweeten. Add salt and pepper to taste.

Pour the dressing over the salad and mix. I like to leave it to stand for at least an hour to let the vegetables absorb the dressing's flavours. Serve with toasted pumpkin seeds sprinkled over the top. This will keep in the fridge for 2 days and is great for lunch the next day.

TIP
This makes a good accompaniment to our Chicken Burger (page 64).

BAKED BEANS

We're all keen to cut down on the sugar in our diet and these baked beans are the ideal fit. They store well in the fridge and are good to eat at any time of day. Definitely one for the whole family.

SERVES 2

1 tsp Lucy Bee coconut oil
1 x 400g tin/1⅓ cups cannellini beans, drained and rinsed
1 x 400g tin/2 cups chopped tomatoes
1 tsp maple syrup
1 tsp paprika
Lucy Bee Himalayan salt and ground black pepper

Heat the coconut oil in a frying pan, add the cannellini beans and stir, then add the tomatoes, maple syrup and paprika. Bring to the boil, stirring frequently, then turn the heat down and simmer for a further 5 minutes, still stirring frequently. Add salt and pepper to taste.

TIP
These can be eaten hot or cold.

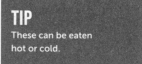

GLUTEN-FREE PASTRY

Finally, we've cracked gluten-free pastry! For anyone who has tried to make this in the past you'll know how difficult it is. It crumbles, falls apart and is not your friend. But, after lots of attempts and years of trying this recipe finally works. Hurrah!

MAKES APPROX 400G/ 14 OZ PASTRY

90g/3 oz Lucy Bee coconut oil (not too hard)
250g/1¾ cups plus 2 tbsp gluten-free plain (all-purpose) flour
¼ tsp xanthan gum
Pinch of Lucy Bee Himalayan salt
2 egg yolks
5 tbsp cold water

Put the coconut oil, flour, xanthan gum and salt into a food processer and blitz until the mixture resembles breadcrumbs. Add the egg yolks and cold water and blitz again until it comes together and forms a dough. Remove and mould briefly into a round then wrap in cling film and chill in the fridge for 15 minutes. Preheat the oven to 200°C/400°F/gas mark 6.

Roll out the chilled pastry between two sheets of cling film until about 3mm/1⅛ in thick and big enough to line a loose-based 23cm/9 in diameter fluted tart tin. Gently peel off the top sheet of cling film and carefully invert the pastry into the tin. Remove the second sheet of cling film and press the pastry gently into the fluted edges of the tin. If the pastry tears a little, use your fingers to gently mould the pastry into the gaps. Neaten off the top edge of the pastry using a knife and place in the freezer to chill for 5 minutes.

Remove the pastry from the freezer and line with baking parchment and ceramic baking beans. Blind bake in the middle of the oven for 10–15 minutes until the pastry just begins to colour, then remove the baking beans and parchment and return the pastry case to the oven for a further 5 minutes, to cook the base. Remove and leave the pastry case to cool in the tin before adding your filling. This freezes well.

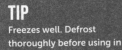

TIP
Freezes well. Defrost thoroughly before using in a recipe.

SWEET CHILLI DIPPING SAUCE

Try our lower natural sugar version of a sweet chilli dipping sauce.

MAKES ABOUT 125ML/½ CUP

1 red pepper (bell pepper), quartered and deseeded
2 garlic cloves, peeled
2 red chillies (seeds left in if you like it spicy), roughly chopped
1 large tomato, quartered
3 tbsp white wine vinegar
6 tbsp runny honey
Lucy Bee Himalayan salt and ground black pepper

Blitz the (bell) pepper, garlic, chillies and tomato together in food processor, or chop very finely by hand, then stir in the vinegar, honey and a pinch each of salt and pepper. Pour the mixture into a small frying pan and place over a high heat until it bubbles and is heated through, then lower the heat and simmer the sauce to reduce for 10 minutes or so. Taste, adjust the seasoning if needed, then leave to cool.

TIP
Add more chilli if you prefer a spicier flavour. You can also add a little cornflour (cornstarch) for a thicker consistency.

GF WF LF DF V VEG   GF WF LF DF V VEG

NUTRITIONAL
INFORMATION

ALMONDS are high in heart-healthy monounsaturated fats. **Almond flour** is a good gluten-free baking ingredient and keeps cakes deliciously moist. **Almond milk** is my favourite dairy-free option to add to breakfasts and smoothies or shakes. It also happens to be a good source of protein and is rich in riboflavin, a form of vitamin B that is proven to work with other nutrients to regulate muscle strength and growth. Almond milk may even give you glowing skin and hair, thanks to its vitamin E content.

ANCHOVIES pack in a lot of flavour for such a small fish, so you only need to use a small amount. They are rich in omega-3s, which can prevent inflammation, and also rich in magnesium and calcium, for strong bones and teeth.

APRICOTS, dried, are an ideal way to increase your dietary fibre intake as well potassium, iron and antioxidants.

ASPARAGUS is a great way to get in your dosage of folate, vitamins A, C, E and K, and chromium.

AUBERGINES (EGGPLANTS) are packed with vitamins, minerals and fibre, as well as being rich in antioxidants, such as nasunin, which gives aubergine its purple colour and can protect the fats in brain cell membranes.

AVOCADO is one of the most nutritious foods you'll ever come across. Rich in healthy fats to reduce inflammation, it's high in fibre and vitamins such as K, C and E, and is also loaded with potassium. It can even help you to absorb nutrients from other plant-based foods.

BANANAS are great for your body and can aid digestion, as well as giving you a real bounce in energy. The potassium can protect against muscle cramps.

BASIL has antibacterial as well as anti-inflammatory properties, which are great for reducing swelling, and is known to have anti-ageing properties. It is also a good way to get your vitamin A, which can protect from free radicals.

BAY LEAVES are great for the digestion, and have the ability to detoxify and reduce inflammation.

BEETROOT (BEETS) lends the most beautiful purple colour to dishes and is also incredibly good for you. It contains a unique group of antioxidants known as betacyanins (which happen to give it the vibrant colour), and it also supports the liver, purifies the blood and improves circulation.

BICARBONATE OF SODA isn't just a great home remedy for teeth whitening, insect bites and as a natural deodorant, it also neutralizes stomach acid to treat heartburn and indigestion.

BROCCOLI is extremely good for you. It has a blend of phytonutrients and is high in mood-boosting vitamin D. It also contains a certain flavonoid which can lessen the impact of allergies and reactions on the body. And one serving can give you 150% of your daily dose of vitamin C.

BROWN RICE is far healthier than white rice, which has been stripped of all goodness and nutrients during the refining process. Brown rice is also high in selenium, which cuts the risk of developing diseases such as heart disease, as well as manganese, which helps the body to process fats. The fibre content also helps to keep you feeling fuller for longer.

BROWN RICE PASTA, my favourite gluten-free pasta, tastes every bit as delicious as the less healthy white kind. Made from just brown rice and water, it contains the same nutrients and health benefits of rice and so is an excellent source of manganese for energy production, selenium for immune function, and magnesium, which helps to ease muscle aches and sleep problems such as insomnia.

BRUSSELS SPROUTS are a great way to get in some vitamins C and K: just one serving will give you your recommended daily allowance.

CACAO doesn't just taste delicious, it's extremely high in antioxidants, magnesium and flavanols and other components found in cacao can lower blood pressure and boost circulation. It's also a known mood-booster, while the ancient Aztecs would even use it as an aphrodisiac.

CANNELLINI BEANS are good for bulking up dishes. They have an incredibly low GI, which means they keep you feeling full for hours, giving you energy long after you've eaten. The beans are also thought to have a detoxifying effect on the body, while being super-charged with antioxidants.

CAPERS are rich in the antioxidant quercetin, which has antibacterial and anti-inflammatory properties. They also give you a healthy dose of vitamins A and K.

CARDAMOM is deliciously fragrant and was used for centuries in Ayurvedic medicine as a treatment for mouth ulcers and digestive problems, amongst other things. It's also great for detoxifying the

body as it helps to eliminate waste, and can even freshen the breath too!

CASHEWS and **CASHEW NUT BUTTER** are high in essential amino acids, heart-friendly monounsaturated fats, and minerals, particularly manganese, potassium, copper, iron, magnesium, zinc and selenium.

CAULIFLOWER is full of healthy nutrients and vitamins, including vitamins C, K and B6, and is anti-inflammatory, which helps the body to stay healthy. It is also a great source of omega-3 fatty acids and dietary fibre, and has been found to protect the lining of your stomach.

CHICKPEAS (GARBANZO BEANS), so versatile and high in nutritional value, are one of the cheapest ingredients you can buy. They are high in both fibre and protein, and have a low GI, so work as a slow-release energy source.

CHILLI FLAKES are great for adding a kick to any dish, and they are also known to boost the metabolism and control appetite. They can even reduce pain, thanks to their levels of capsaicin, which can reduce pain-signalling neurotransmitters in the brain to work like a painkiller.

CHIVES are nutrient-dense and contain choline, which can help to aid sleep and relax the muscles.

CIDER VINEGAR is an ancient remedy for all sorts of ailments. It's high in acetic acid, which is antimicrobial and can kill certain bacteria.

CINNAMON is known to be a good anti-inflammatory. It packs a hefty antioxidant punch, with natural antimicrobial properties. It is a natural sweetener.

COCONUT AMINOS are free from gluten and soy, with a low GI, and are high in amino acids, the building blocks of protein. Use in place of soy sauce or tamari in recipes.

COCONUT MILK is perfect for anyone with a dairy allergy. It's also high in a medium-chain saturated fatty acid (MCFA) called lauric acid, which is both antiviral and antibacterial. It is quickly turned into energy by the liver, meaning that it is less likely to be stored as fat by the body.

COCONUT SUGAR, from the coconut palm, is one of the most delicious natural sweeteners on the planet, adding an almost caramel-like taste to foods. Although it's relatively high in carbs and calories, it has a lower GI than some other sugars and tends to have less of an impact on your blood sugar levels. It's also far lower in fructose – a type of sugar which your body converts to fat quickly – than other sweeteners such as agave, and contains nutrients removed in refined sugar, such as iron, zinc, calcium and potassium. **Desiccated coconut** is a great way to sweeten dishes in a healthier way and I'll even use it in cakes and bakes to add flavour. It's also rich in iron and fibre.

COD is a great way of getting lean protein into your diet. It's a good source of my favourite omega-3s, known to keep your heart healthy, as well as of selenium and vitamin B12.

CORIANDER (CILANTRO) can be used to treat inflamed skin, lower cholesterol and blood pressure, and also to strengthen the bones, owing to its calcium content.

CORNFLOUR (CORNSTARCH) is a good alternative in gluten-free cooking. It's high in fibre and iron, and also contains phosphorus, which supports healthy enzyme function.

COURGETTES (ZUCCHINI) make healthy living so much easier and more exciting. They are a good source of folates, which are beneficial to the foetus during pregnancy. They're also a great way to get heart-healthy potassium into your diet, which can help to reduce blood pressure.

CUMIN, like cardamom, can be used to help with digestion, as it activates the salivary glands. It's even thought to be a natural remedy for insomnia because its vitamin complex can help to relax and induce sleep.

DARK CHOCOLATE is a great source of antioxidants and magnesium.

DATES are not only nature's sweets, they can help to relieve digestive problems such as constipation, while the minerals found in dates can help to boost bone and tooth strength. The iron content is also great for those who suffer from anaemia.

EDAMAME BEANS are a good source of protein, fibre, amino acids as well as minerals such as magnesium, iron, zinc and potassium.

EGGS are an inexpensive source of high-quality protein. Both the white and yolk are rich in vitamins and minerals, and the yolk is full of omega-3 fatty acids. They are also an excellent source of phosphorus, selenium, vitamins A, B2, B5 and B12, as well as choline, an important nutrient for brain function.

FENNEL is great for heart health as it contains fibre, potassium, vitamins C and B6 and is

cholesterol-free. Its distinctive aniseed flavour is a great addition to many dishes.

FENUGREEK has long been used as a medicinal remedy in parts of Asia. It contains muscle-building protein, vitamin C, potassium and diosgenin.

FETA is made with sheep or goat's milk and has a strong, salty taste, which means less is more. It's a great way to get calcium into your diet, and it's also rich in vitamin B12, for red blood cell production.

FLAXSEED is high in heart-healthy omega-3s, and also contains both soluble and insoluble fibre.

GARLIC isn't just for scaring vampires! In fact, it's full of body-loving benefits and is great for fighting off colds and flu too. It can also help to improve iron metabolism, and may help to lower blood pressure, or hypertension.

GINGER is the perfect home remedy for treating nausea and sickness – particularly good for mums-to-be – but can also help to ease symptoms of colic. Its anti-inflammatory properties also make it ideal for helping with joint or muscle pain, as well as coughs and colds.

GOJI BERRIES are small, red berries that protect against heart disease and contain vitamins C, B2 and A, plus iron and antioxidants.

HALLOUMI is high in calcium and is also a good source of protein for vegetarians.

HAZELNUTS are naturally sweet and tasty but are also incredibly nutritious, too. They are extremely high in energy (great for a pre- or post-workout snack)

and monounsaturated fatty acids and essential fatty acid. As a great source of vitamin E, they're also perfect for making the skin glow.

HEMP SEEDS are wonderful for an energy boost – a perfect pre- or post-workout addition – and also high in protein.

LAMB, particularly grass-fed lamb, is surprisingly high in omega-3s and also omega-6 fatty acid and conjugated linoleic acid (CLA), which can boost the immune system.

LEMONS are a natural immune booster and great for easing the symptoms of coughs, colds and sore throats. They increase the body's iron absorption and can give you glowing, healthy skin.

LENTILS are not only a cheap way to bulk up meals, they're also high in nutrients, and a great way for vegetarians or vegans to get their protein. They give plenty of slow-release energy, and are low in fat and calories. They can also be used to lower cholesterol, improve digestion and increase energy levels.

LIME is a citrus juice full of vitamin C, great at fighting off diseases and cold viruses, and can even help to give fresh, glowing skin. Lime also aids digestion and can relieve constipation.

LUCUMA, a caramel-like sweetener that tastes similar to maple syrup, makes an amazing alternative to processed sugars. It has a low GI and many other health benefits too, including being high in antioxidants, fibre and anti-inflammatories.

MANGO is wonderful at helping to clear up the skin and is also high in vitamin A, which is great for eye health. It can also normalize blood sugar levels and improve digestion, thanks to a series of enzymes that can break down proteins.

MANUKA HONEY, from New Zealand, is by far the most superior of the many honeys on the market. It has antibacterial and healing properties and works wonders in fighting bugs and other nasties. It's also high in antioxidants to protect us against free radicals.

MAPLE SYRUP is a perfect option for anyone with a sweet tooth. It's high in nutrients, including magnesium, potassium, zinc and calcium.

MINT is brilliant for indigestion as it can soothe the stomach and also encourages the salivary glands to secrete digestive enzymes. It's also great for treating congestion – perfect for when you're bunged up and full of cold.

MOZZARELLA is a great source of protein, fantastic for energy levels and building muscle, but is also rich in bone-strengthening calcium and skin- and vision-loving niacin, riboflavin, thiamine, biotin and vitamin B6.

MUSSELS are high in vitamins, including B12, B and C, and are also a good source of iron, potassium and zinc.

MUSTARD is full of health benefits, and known to ease muscle aches and pains, as well as symptoms of psoriasis and respiratory problems. The seeds are high in omega-3s and contain phytonutrients, while the selenium and magnesium found in them have anti-inflammatory effects.

NIGELLA seeds, also called black cumin, have for centuries been one of the most widely used medicinal seeds. The ancient Greek physician Dioscorides used them to treat headaches and toothaches. They're also commonly used to aid digestion, and they can even be used as a treatment for psoriasis and for eczema.

OATS are not only cheap to buy but they're also the perfect breakfast food as they're fantastic at fuelling the body and keeping you feeling full. Oats contain a special kind of fibre, which can lower cholesterol levels and stabilize blood sugar levels, meaning they can prevent huge spikes in blood sugar levels. They are also a great source of magnesium.

OLIVE OIL contains about 75% oleic acid, which aids in balancing cholesterol in the body. The quality of olive oil affects its benefits so it's worth opting for the best available where possible.

PAK CHOI (BOK CHOY), is a leafy Chinese cabbage which is popular in health circles because of its phytonutrients, vitamins and health-boosting antioxidants. It is also rich in potassium and iron.

PAPRIKA offers a whole host of health benefits. It's high in beta-carotene, which the body converts into the skin-loving and wrinkle-zapping vitamin A. It can even be used in homemade face masks, to reduce fine lines and leave skin glowing!

PARSLEY is rich in many vital vitamins, including C, B12, K and A, meaning that it is wonderful for keeping the immune system strong and strengthening your bones and nervous system.

PARSNIPS are rich in vitamins, dietary fibre and minerals.

PEAS contain lots of phytonutrients with antioxidant and anti-inflammatory benefits, including some which are exclusively found in these little green gems. They also contain omega-3 fats in the form of ALAs, and plenty of vitamin E and beta-carotene for healthy skin and eyes.

PECANS are lovely and buttery in baking and are a great source of energy. They are rich in fatty acids and also contain vitamin E to rid the body of toxic free radicals and protect from diseases.

PINEAPPLE has been used for centuries to treat digestive problems and inflammation. It is high in antioxidants such as vitamins C, beta-carotene and the minerals copper, zinc and folate.

PINE NUTS are naturally sweet and delicious, but are also a good source of plant-derived nutrients, vitamins and minerals, as well as heart-healthy monounsaturated fatty acids. Their high vitamin E content makes them great for the skin.

POMEGRANATES are like nature's rubies – they just look so beautiful when added to dishes. This nutrient-dense and antioxidant-rich fruit (the most powerful of all the fruits) is also an ancient symbol of fertility and health.

POTATOES can have quite a bad reputation, with most people in health and fitness circles avoiding them. However, they can help to fight inflammation and are even known to lower blood pressure. They're also rich in vitamin B6, which can build cells and support the body's nervous system.

PRAWNS (SHRIMP) are a fantastic source of protein, and good at boosting our omega-3 levels.

PUMPKIN SEEDS are a tasty source of vitamin B and iron.

QUINOA, actually a pseudo-cereal, is a great option for anyone with a gluten intolerance, and is one of my favourite healthy carbs. It's a brilliant source of protein, fatty acids, as well as B vitamins, magnesium and calcium. It is a fibre-rich whole grain, and so wonderful for digestion.

RAISINS are a wonderful high-energy food that contain high levels of the antioxidant catechin.

RASPBERRIES are lower in sugar than many fruits but also provide you with plenty of vitamin C and other antioxidants. They are also high in flavonoids.

RED WINE contains tannins, which are what gives the wine its colour. It's known to protect against heart disease.

ROCKET (ARUGULA) is packed with vital phytochemicals, vitamins and minerals. It's also a wonderful source of folates and vitamin C, helping to protect from disease.

ROSEMARY is great at improving digestion and is full of anti-inflammatory and antioxidant compounds.

SALMON is packed full of goodness and body-loving properties. It's high in omega-3s and is also a good source of skin-boosting vitamin E. It's also a wonderful source of lean protein for muscle building and repair, and contains essential amino acids and vitamins A, D, B6 and B.

SESAME OIL and **SESAME SEEDS** are packed with magnesium as well as zinc, which is essential for producing collagen to smooth out wrinkles and plump up the skin. Sesame is also one of the best sources of calcium on the planet. **Tahini**, a paste made from sesame seeds, is one of my favourite ingredients and I love to add it to dressings and sauces for an added health boost.

SHALLOTS generally have a higher mineral content than your typical onion. They are also high in antioxidants, which are released when the shallot is crushed or sliced, and contain iron to boost energy, cell regrowth, healing and metabolism.

SPINACH is one of those leafy greens that just keeps on giving, full of body-loving boosters. I like to add handfuls to all sorts of meals – including green smoothies – since it is so high in vitamin C and full of anti-inflammatories and antioxidants. Adding spinach to your diet is also a great way to dose up on vitamin K, which is good for strong bones. It's also a wonderful source of energy, contains folic acid, and can improve the quality of the blood, thanks to its high iron content.

SULTANAS come from red grapes, so are high in antioxidants such as resveratrol, which has been found to be anti-inflammatory, as well as fighting against certain cancers and lowering bad cholesterol.

SUNFLOWER SEEDS are a good way to get folate in pregnancy.

SWEET POTATOES are one of the healthiest foods on the planet. They're an excellent source of vitamin C and are also rich in vitamin D, which boosts the immune system, helps to raise energy levels, and can even make us feel happier. Their high vitamin E content is good for fresh, youthful skin, and their beta-carotene is antioxidant and antiviral.

THYME is a good source of vitamins C and A, iron, manganese, copper and dietary fibre. It's also believed to fight bacteria found in foods.

TOFU (BEANCURD) is an ideal vegan source of protein as it contains all eight essential amino acids. It is also high in iron and calcium, as well as manganese, selenium, phosphorous, magnesium and zinc.

TOMATOES are incredibly nutrient-dense and contain an array of nutrients and antioxidants, including alpha-lipoic acid, which helps to convert glucose to energy, and lycopene, which helps to protect against free radicals. They are also a good source of vitamins A and C, as well as folic acid, making them the perfect staple for pregnant women.

TURKEY is very lean and the high levels of protein will keep you full for hours. It also contains selenium.

TURMERIC is a super-spice and a traditional remedy for all sorts of ailments. It contains curcumin, a powerful antioxidant that has strong anti-inflammatory effects.

VANILLA PODS AND SEEDS come from the tropical climbing orchid and contain small amounts of B vitamins and magnesium, calcium, zinc and iron.

WALNUTS are packed with omega-3 fatty acids – great for glowing skin and hair.

INDEX

THANK YOU

A massive thank you to my family – **mum Natalie, dad Phil, sister Daisy and brother Jack** – for always being so supportive and caring and teaching me so much before and since working at Lucy Bee. You have made so many opportunities happen and have always made sure that myself, Daisy and Jack are happy in what we are doing and always want the best for us. I love the fact we all get to work together and how busy and exciting it is working at Lucy Bee. Thanks for your input with the recipes too.

Petrina Grint – Thank you for all your hard work and being my left and right arm throughout both books. You are so caring and make this very stressful time a lot easier for everyone with your support, kindness and organisation. It wouldn't be the same without you being here 24/7 and we are lucky to have you on the team! **Megan Phizacklea** – I have loved every minute of recipe creating and testing with you. It's been so much fun and never feels like work when I'm around you. I am so lucky that we get to do all of this together – we should be proud of what we've achieved. You always give me the best advice and I know you'll always make me feel better when I'm worried or nervous about anything. Can't wait for all the exciting times to come! (HashtagLucy&Meg). **Hannah Grint** – My writing partner in crime and general mood booster. It's non-stop laughing when I'm with you and I'm happy that I got to share this experience with you before you head off on a new career path, my sister from another mister! **Georgia Hyne** – It's great having you on board. Thanks for all your hard work so far and I can't wait for what's still to come. I'm so happy you've joined the Lucy Bee team. You are always so supportive and I love how passionate you are about the brand! **Helena Wood** – Gee whizz, you sure know how to rustle up some great cakes and pastries. Thank you for all your delicious masterpieces in this book. Exciting times ahead for you – so talented! I love you being part of the team! PS, I'm loving the gluten-free and dairy-free profiteroles! **Sadika Ekemen** – Bringing a 'Turkish twist' to this cookbook. Thanks to you and your mum for your recipes. I LOVE Turkish food so thanks for letting us use these in the book. I'm so excited you've joined the team with your artistic flare – you're a great person to be around. Roll on many more fun times! **Richard Willis** – For testing out the majority of the food (with no complaint I might add!). Thank you for giving me the best, most caring and honest advice. You are always there when I need to laugh, cry, stress, or when I just really need a drink. **Sarah Pearce** – Gluten-free cheese straws? YUM! Thank you for sharing some fantastic recipes with us. Coming up with great gluten-free pastry that's easy to use is a winner. I know that coeliacs and anyone else wanting to avoid wheat and gluten will be very happy! **Karl Brown** – aka the Trainer. We all love you for keeping us motivated and positive 24/7. Your laugh is infectious and you're the best person to be around! **Ash Buckingham** – Thanks for sharing your artistic creativity with food! **Edward Palmer** – For always being there whenever we need help with anything! **Jim Kinloch** and **Ollie Scales** – For making sure we are making the most out of everything in the IT world. Ollie it's great having you on board! **Sarah Waller** – It's lovely having you here and I'm looking forward to working with you more in the future!

Dan Jones – Incredible photography! Thank you for all your hard work. Every photo ended up being my 'favourite'! **Sophie Fox** – Loved all of our chats on health while you helped Dan snap the excellent photos! **Bianca Nice** – Blown away at your organisation and super speedy talent in making the photos look stunning. Most photos I just want to nose dive into the page and eat! Loved spending time with you on set while we shot them. **Tamara Vos** and **Jenna Leiter** – Thank you for helping Bianca in making the food look gorgeous in the book. Great working with you again Jenna. Looking forward to the launch! **Maria Comparetto** – Thank you for the beautiful make-up! **Amy Christian** – Thank you for all your hard work, keeping everything calm and helping us step-by-step making sure this book is perfect and up to the standard we wanted it to be. **Katherine Keeble** – Thank you so much for putting the book together and making it look so beautiful. It's always lovely spending time with you while shooting the books. Thank you everyone at **Quadrille** for making the books happen.

Lucy Bee followers – Thank you for your loyalty and support. Lucy Bee wouldn't be the same without you all and we are lucky to have such lovely people sending in photos of their meals and how they use Lucy Bee for cooking, for their pets or for beauty. You keep us positive and excited!

 x